Winning IN BOTH LEAGUES

Winning

IN BOTH LEAGUES

REFLECTIONS FROM BASEBALL'S FRONT OFFICE

J. Frank Cashen

Foreword by BILLY BEANE

UNIVERSITY OF NEBRASKA PRESS Lincoln and London

Library of Congress
Cataloging-in-Publication Data
Cashen, J. Frank.
Winning in both leagues: reflections from
baseball's front office / J. Frank Cashen;
foreword by Billy Beane.
pages   cm
ISBN 978-0-8032-4965-3 (cloth: alk. paper)
ISBN 978-0-8032-6544-8 (epub)
ISBN 978-0-8032-6545-5 (mobi)
ISBN 978-0-8032-6546-2 (pdf)
1. Cashen, J. Frank. 2. Baseball teams—
United States—Management. 3. Major
League Baseball (Organization) 4. New
York Mets (Baseball team) 5. Baltimore
Orioles (Baseball team) I. Title.
GV865.C34A3 2014   796.357092—dc23
[B]
2014006362

Set in Charter ITC Pro and Giza

Contents

Foreword

There is a lot to be learned from how Frank Cashen put together a Major League Baseball team. Few have done it better. He built a foundation through the amateur draft and then finished it off with shrewd player trades.

Sandy Alderson was my mentor with the Oakland Athletics, but it was Frank Cashen who inspired me to become a general manager when I was a young player with the New York Mets.

Frank is one of the few baseball executives to win the World Series in both leagues—first with the Baltimore Orioles in the American League and then with the New York Mets in the National League. Cashen did all this after being an award-winning writer, the operator of two race tracks, and a "big leaguer" in the advertising world.

The Orioles were good when he arrived and even better when he left. The Mets were at the bottom when he arrived and consistent contenders when he left. Along with Darryl Strawberry and John Gibbons, I was near the top of the first amateur draft that he put together in New York, and thus I witnessed personally how the Mets' rebuilding began.

His Mets teams were the best in all of baseball in the 1980s, and the Hall of Fame in Cooperstown is filled with the players who made that possible. The numbers of those Mets stars are exceeded only by an earlier group from his Baltimore Orioles teams of the late 1960s and 1970s. No one will forget the Robinsons (Frank and Brooks), Jim Palmer, or the irrepressible Earl Weaver, whom Cashen nominates as the best baseball manager of all time.

In addition to his chronicle of these great baseball years, Cashen takes you back to his Baltimore boyhood, his numerous and varied careers, and even a personal journey to Ireland and Italy. In fact, *Winning in Both Leagues* is filled with journeys of all kinds and you will find it impossible to put down.

> *Billy Beane*
> *General Manager, Oakland Athletics*

Preface

In the pages that follow is the story of my improbable journey through the world of baseball from the mid-1960s to the early 1990s.

As I grow older, I realize that great memories are among my most cherished possessions.

After I wrote that line in answering a letter from an old friend, I got to thinking and remembering and reminiscing and wondering. I wondered whether it was worth writing down. That brought to mind Jack Batty, a local scribe in our neighbor- hood in Easton, Maryland, a product of General Electric's public relations group. He had put together a description of me that was as accurate as anything I had ever seen. "Cashen was," he wrote, "a writer and a newspaperman by choice, a lawyer by education, a race track operator by heritage, brewery executive by dollar necessity, advertising manager by curiosity, marketing and sales official by progression, and baseball general manager by good fortune."

What a great bunch of jobs. How incredible it all was. And I never had difficulty holding a single one of them.

Let's tackle baseball, the good fortune part, first. Jerry Hoffberger, the head of the National Brewing Company in Baltimore, picked me for several of these jobs.

He had hired me out of the newspaper business to work at a harness track his family operated, the old Baltimore Raceway. Shortly thereafter, the Hoffbergers acquired the thoroughbred Bel Air track in nearby Harford County and I ended up operating both. Several assignments later, I had a top-grade position as director of advertising for the several breweries that National Brewery then owned. It was from this position that, quite unexpectedly, my career in baseball began. Come with me as we journey through baseball history—from the mid-1960s to the early 1990s—as seen by one who lived it and loved it.

Acknowledgments

To my wife, Jean Cashen, who has put up with me for
sixty-plus years, and Jack Batty, a neighbor and friend,
without whom this book would never have been possible.
I am also indebted to Beverly Kohlhepp, E Dee Merriken
Monnen, Marc and Vivienne Jaffe, and Victor Tempkin for
their help and timely advice along the way.

Winning IN BOTH LEAGUES

Beating Boston

Most baseball fans remember 1986 not as the year the New York Mets won the World Series but rather the time Bill Buckner and the Boston Red Sox snatched defeat from the jaws of victory. For me, as the general manager, and for Mets fans, that sweet victory capped six years of rebuilding the club that became a memorable winner.

And while the Red Sox Nation faced a winter of discontent, and Bill Buckner a decade of abuse, New Yorkers rejoiced over the end of a rare drought in baseball championships. The Yankees had last done it in 1978 and the Mets' only world championship had occurred a whole generation earlier, in 1969.

The World Series win was a great moment for the team and the fans. For me, it was the pinnacle of my long and very fortunate career in baseball. But it almost didn't happen that way, as any baseball observer in 1986 may well remember. I know I will.

What happened in Game Six of that World Series on October 25, 1986, was historic, and worth describing again in some detail.

Down three games to two, the Mets headed from Boston to New York for Game Six. We were in a tough spot, having just lost Game Five at Fenway Park, with our ace, Dwight Gooden, on the mound. We faced elimination from our championship dreams. Friday was an off day, the traditional travel day, and twenty-four hours more to worry and fret. It wasn't just the Saturday game, but we also needed the one after that for the title. The Mets were going to have to win the next two on their home field at Shea Stadium.

A young Roger Clemens was on the mound for Boston, facing the Mets' Bob Ojeda. The Sox held a 2–0 lead in the bottom of the fifth, when we struck back with two to tie. Boston then scored and led 3–2 in the seventh. But the Mets tied it, 3–3, on Gary Carter's sacrifice fly in the bottom of the eighth. The score remained tied through the ninth, forcing the game into extra innings. Boston scored two in the top of the tenth to lead 5–3. Things looked bleak for the home team.

From my box in the press section, I could see the excitement growing in the Red Sox dugout. My friend Lou Gorman, the general manager of the Red Sox, had escorted Boston owner Mrs. Tom Yawkey down next to the Red Sox dugout to be ready to enter the locker room to celebrate with her new world champions. Mrs. Yawkey, of course, was the gracious lady who owned the Red Sox after her husband, the legendary Tom Yawkey, passed away. Knowing how Lou would have the champagne iced for the festivities, I must admit the thought crossed my mind that as long as we weren't going to win the big prize, I was glad Gorman and his Red Sox would. He and I had been associates too long, too many times, to think otherwise.

As that final inning started, I went to Mets owner Nelson Doubleday's box and suggested that we go down to the Red Sox locker room, after they had clinched it, to congratulate Mrs. Yawkey, Lou Gorman, and the rest on winning the World Series.

"You don't have to stay long," I told him, "in fact, you shouldn't. There will be some pictures, but it's their celebration and we should get out in a hurry."

Doubleday said no and continued, "Frank, you handle it. You've done everything else to get us here and you can certainly express our congratulations." So Fred Wilpon, who at that time was club president, agreed to go with me. We stood in the back of the press box to watch what looked like the last half inning of the game. I had already instructed the elevator operator to hold the elevator for us because it would be in great demand once the game was over. What happened next will always be remembered by those who were either present, listening on the radio, or watching on TV.

Our first two batters, Wally Backman and Keith Hernandez, were quickly retired in the bottom of the tenth and the Red Sox were one out away from their first World Series Championship since 1918, ending the so-called Curse of the Bambino (punishment upon the Sox for the infamous sale of Babe Ruth to the hated Yankees). Down to our last out, the Mets rose from the dead when Gary Carter, Kevin Mitchell, and Ray Knight all singled to move the Mets within a run of the Sox. Both Carter and Knight got their hits when down to their last strikes. This brought center fielder Mookie Wilson to the plate. A wild pitch by Boston reliever Bob Stanley got Mitchell home to tie the contest as the Shea Stadium crowd turned delirious. Wilson, still at bat, then hit what was best described as a dribbler toward first base. Fleet-footed, Wilson took off like a rocket down the first base line. Playing just off first { 3 base, Bill Buckner, perhaps distracted by Mookie's blazing speed, let the ball go through his legs. As Wilson stepped safely on the first base bag, Knight romped home with the winning run and the Mets survived what looked to be a sure defeat. People who saw that game will remember it to their dying day.

When Wilson landed on first base, I was stunned. The crowd started to bellow, then broke into a full-throated roar that didn't stop. On the contrary, it seemed to grow in intensity, and the whole park was soon on its feet, screaming. I later realized that the considerable numbers of Boston fans still in the ballpark were crying in dismay, while the locals were in a high state of elation. Feeding the latter was the show on the field as Mets players thumped each other, jumped on top of each other, and generally behaved like an unruly bunch of juveniles. But after watching the scene on the playing field, I realized that the people in the sky boxes and the ones in the grandstand were not acting dissimilarly.

Coming off that Saturday night high was no small challenge either. The seventh and deciding game was scheduled for the

next night. Those twenty-four hours to that seventh and deciding game had to be the longest day and night of my life. The day
started unpromising to say the least: rainy, windy, gloomy. Would
it clear in time for the game? That was the first question that came
to mind when I staggered out of bed after the previous night's
short session of drinking and celebrating that come-from-behind
victory. No answer being relevant, it did call for an early return to
the ballpark, where the worrying only gathered more intensity.

The hope for a game that night gradually faded as the weather
showed no signs of letting up, and radio and television and a
half-hundred newspaper people were clamoring for a decision.
The commissioner finally called the game and put off the showdown until the following night. Another twenty-four hours to
wait. The World Series had to be over that next day, or, to be
exact, the next night.

4 }   No matter the outcome, it would mean the final bolt would be
driven in my six-year rebuilding job of moving the Mets from the
worst organization in the big leagues to the very best. Actually,
the club had been turned around two years earlier—in 1984, when
the Mets finished with a 90-72 record, their first above .500 since
1976. But here we were in October 1986, still short of the world
championship. What about a loss in the now-delayed seventh
game? Such a loss would mean all those hopes and dreams would
come up short. Still, I thought, it would have been an interesting
and cherished journey, but lacking the gold at the end of the
rainbow. Honestly, I was so focused on winning that I gave scant
consideration to the prospect of losing.

And for the chief executive of the Mets, there were other game-
related concerns at hand. Would the playing field be dried out for
the Monday finale? The infield was covered with a tarp, but the rest
of the field was totally exposed. There was a legion of ticket and
hotel reservation problems prompted principally by the postponed
game. The vast majority of the problems involved season ticket
holders and other baseball teams. For customers of that stripe you

always moved mountains. All of these problems seemed to run together and left their residue in my throat and stomach. Would these twenty-four hours, now forty-eight, ever end?

For the Boston press, it was another day to vilify Bill Buckner, which turned into weeks, which turned into months, and, yes, into years. Bill, who lived in New England, put up with it for as long as he could, but to protect his family he escaped Boston and relocated to Idaho, where the 1986 World Series was not as memorable an event. Years later, twenty-two to be exact, the Boston team invited him back and sought to make amends. Belatedly, he was cheered with a standing ovation at Fenway Park. It may have been forgiven but it never has been forgotten.

My own opinion is that the whole matter was blown grossly out of proportion. Fair-minded baseball people will tell you that Wilson was most likely going to beat the ball out for a base hit and it didn't make any difference what Buckner did. Bill Buckner was a good ballplayer (he compiled a lifetime batting average of .289 over twenty-one seasons in the Majors) and an all-around good guy. I said it then and I have never changed my mind.

Boston had its best pitcher, Bruce Hurst, on the mound for Game Seven. The Sox picked up three runs in the second inning off our starter, Ron Darling, and held onto that lead until the bottom of the sixth, when New York got three of its own. Hernandez drove in two and Knight, who was having a dream series, homered in the seventh to put the Mets up for keeps. Hernandez drove in another run and Darryl Strawberry cracked a home run for an 8–5 lead. Roger McDowell got the win, with help from closer Jesse Orosco—and the Mets were world champions. What a moment after our improbable recovery from near death on Saturday night! It was great to have helped produce a winner, and an unforgettable time to be a part of the national pastime.

Winning the World Series, I couldn't help but reflect on my years in baseball and how it all started, and what an unlikely journey it was.

Call from the Boss

It was the fall of 1965. I was sitting in my office at National Brewing when my intercom buzzed and a woman's voice I recognized asked, "Busy?" It was Jerry Hoffberger's secretary. Sometimes that's a loaded question, especially when it comes in the middle of the workday. Be careful how you answer it. "Not particularly, what's up?" was my reply. "The boss would like to see you," she said. The boss, of course, was Jerry Hoffberger, CEO of National Brewing Company, where I had happily toiled as advertising director for the past four years. "Coming," I answered and headed from my third-floor office to the first floor of the East Baltimore building, where the executive offices were located.

The Hoffberger family had been prominent in Baltimore for many years. After attending the University of Virginia and serving as a U.S. Army officer in World War II, Jerry Hoffberger was president of the National Brewing Company from 1946 to 1973. He was involved with the Baltimore Orioles from its Major League inception in 1954 as a part-owner and then majority owner from 1965 to 1979. He did similar stints with the Baltimore Colts, at that time the city's entry in the National Football League. A bigger-than-life figure, Jerry was a civic benefactor who gave major contributions to schools and hospitals and was a leader in the city's improving fortunes in the 1970s.

After the usual greetings, Jerry invited me to sit down, then inquired about my assistant, Bill Costello, a very bright young man whom I had hired away from *Life* magazine where he'd been a staff writer. Previously he had been a sportswriter at the *Baltimore Evening Sun*, but having moved away from journalism, he had taken a quick liking to the ad business. It was easy to respond with the usual complimentary remarks, though Hoffberger startled me with his next question: "Is he ready to take your job and run the advertising department?" "I believe so," I answered cautiously, "but why do you ask?"

All kinds of foolish things ran through my mind. "Where had I screwed up?" "Who had complained?" "Who the hell had the right to or the grounds to complain?" No answers came up on the spot, so I turned my full attention to what Jerry had to say. "I'm thinking about a new assignment for you, but first I want to make sure the advertising department is set." "Billy will do fine," I protested, "but what's this stuff about a new assignment?"

Hoffberger spoke dispassionately, sensing that I was a bit confused. First he said he appreciated the report I had submitted earlier on the Orioles and had given it a lot of thought. Then he added that he was convinced in his own mind that the Orioles organization did a poor job of marketing the ball club. It was an area that needed immediate attention. His voice became more positive as he went on to say he felt I could, working with chief executive officer and general manager Lee MacPhail, supply the needed ingredient. I was stunned and had no ready answer.

The report he referred to had come about many months earlier. In early 1965 Jerry was more than certain he was going to have control of the club the following year. In fact, he had discussed it with me. After cautioning me to keep the matter "under my hat," he asked a favor. Pointing out that he was probably a year away from making any changes in the club, he asked me to spend the pending 1965 season closely watching the team—particularly the personnel—and the office group as well.

The Orioles' principal owner at the time was Joe Iglehart, a local investor and leader of a group of Baltimore business leaders, mostly CEOs of their own companies. In addition to Hoffberger, that group also included Zan Kreiger of the Gunther Brewing Company. National Brewing had arranged to buy Iglehart's stock and thus become the dominant partner. Among Iglehart's investments was a sizable interest in the Columbia Broadcasting System (CBS), where he served as treasurer of the corporation. CBS had just bought the New York Yankees from Dan Topping and Del Webb, and Major League Baseball rules prevented any individual or corporation from having a simultaneous interest in two ball clubs. Iglehart, with some degree of reluctance, decided to sell his interest in the Orioles and retain his position with CBS.

(As an aside, it's interesting to note that, unable to produce positive results and hampered by mounting conflicts of interest over individual clubs' television contracts, CBS, which reportedly paid $14 million for the Yankees, put it up for sale a couple years later. George Steinbrenner and a band of limited partners purchased the Yankees for somewhere between $8 and $10 million, of which he reportedly put up only $168,000 of his own money, in what turned out to be one of the greatest sports purchases of all time.)

Having been a sportswriter for some fifteen years and handling the brewery's radio and television rights after that, the operations side of big league baseball was not exactly new to me. So, while still holding my job as director of advertising, I spent 1965 quietly scrutinizing the Baltimore Orioles organization. At the time Hoffberger made his proposal, I was very happy and comfortable in the advertising job, overseeing a $14 million budget. So I had some initial hesitancy. But I accepted the boss's challenge.

Although I didn't realize it at the time, subsequent events showed I was strangely suited for the challenges I would face. First, I knew the game, having played it from an early age. I played it (badly) in college, so badly, in fact, that one of the coaches later declared I was on the team only because they had an extra uniform. I was a second baseman with a weak arm and an even weaker bat. Even so, for six years after I graduated, I put together and played on a good fast-pitch softball team, the Esquires. I was a pitcher, of sorts, on a successful club.

Second, for a year before I joined the Orioles, I had been evaluating the performance of the playing part of that organization as well as that of its front office. By this time I also had graduated with a JD from the University of Maryland School of Law and had passed the Maryland state bar. This proved most valuable, not only in handling player contracts but in negotiating radio and TV pacts as well. I had had some experience with the latter, since, in my previous stint in advertising at the brewery, I had handled all of the sports media work. That law degree also was most helpful in solving professional baseball's labyrinth of rights and rules. Finally, my years as a sportswriter for the *Baltimore News-Post* had given me a good grasp of public and media relations, and as an advertising executive, I was comfortable with sizable budgets and their annual upward climbs.   { 9

With my unusual and eclectic range of experiences and love of baseball, I felt reasonably sure I could tackle Mr. Hoffberger's challenge.

Baltimore Beginnings

It was to be a special privilege to work for the Orioles in Baltimore, my hometown, where my life story began in 1925. Baltimore, remember, was also the birthplace of Babe Ruth. (While I was a pretty good softball player in my youth, my comparison to George Herman Ruth should be limited to our shared birthplace.)

Fourteen years later, after graduating from old St. Paul Parochial School, I very much wanted to attend Mount St. Joseph, a high school run by the Brothers of St. Francis Xavier. A distant, out-of-state cousin of mine had taught there for many years and our family had frequently visited the campus. Everything about the school appealed to me, even though it was on the other side of town in Irvington. I promised my mother I would pay my own tuition if she would agree to St. Joe's, a deal that she readily accepted. And she agreed to provide the streetcar fare—five cents each way.

A full year's tuition back then was sixty dollars, covered in part that year by a Depression-era federal work-study program, which I recall was called the National Youth Administration, or NYA. To make up the difference, I cleaned classrooms and worked in the cafeteria during lunch. At the end of my freshman year, I heard about golf caddying and immediately became enthralled with carrying golf bags around the old Hillendale Country Club on Loch Raven Boulevard. That provided a nice contribution to my tuition fund.

Having encouraged me successfully the previous year, the following spring my mother, Brigid Mary Ryan Cashen, not too long from County Tipperary, Ireland, decided it was time for me to get yet another job and contribute to the family coffers. She had no trouble answering what to me was a difficult question: "Where do I go to look for summer work?" "I'll have a list for you by tomorrow," she promised. And she was as good as her word. The very next morning, before my early journey to St. Joe's, she explained that there were plenty of companies whose products we used, and she would formulate a proper search.

Shortly thereafter she identified two such companies, and she assured me she had at least two more in mind. She proposed that the next week would be the right time to get started. So the following week, as ordered, I got off the No. 8 streetcar on my way home from school and headed for the Western Maryland Dairy in pursuit of a summer job. "We drink a lot of their milk," Brigid Mary reminded me as I went out the door that morning.

I was directed to a very nice, middle-aged (at least that was the opinion of a fifteen-year-old) supervisor from the department closest to the company's front door. He explained that running a dairy was a steady, year-round business and that they "did not have openings" in the summer. But he did not summarily dismiss me. He asked me about school, about what activities I participated in, about my family and a host of other things. Before he let me go, he complimented me for looking for work and we parted like old friends. The experience was very helpful. Going in, I did not know how I would handle talking to older people. I hadn't had any trouble on the golf course, and as it turned out I didn't have any trouble in my job search.

The very next week, the search continued. This time my mother had selected the *Baltimore News-Post* and the *Sunday American*, the local metropolitan newspaper, as the target. I got the usual send-off: "We subscribe to their paper, and if there are any openings, they should hire you." It was the first time I ever heard her say, "If there are any openings." And somehow, it was the most reasonable statement she had made. After a few inquiries, I located

{ 11

the *News-Post* building, three or four blocks on South Street after getting off the No. 8 streetcar halfway home from school. As I was later to learn, if you asked for a transfer, you could use it to make the remainder of the journey on the same five-cent fare.

Once inside the front door of the *News-Post*, I asked the elevator man where I should go to apply for a job. Sensing my less than firm question and noticing, I'm sure, my youthful eagerness, he asked me if I was looking for a job as a newsboy selling papers on the street. I quickly informed him what was on my mind. Shaking his head, he dumped me out on the second floor with the direction to talk to someone in the accounting department. After explaining to the lady at the front desk that I was looking for a summer job, she told me to have a seat and added that somebody would be with me shortly. That somebody turned out to be an interesting-looking gentleman, actually the head of the accounting department, who patiently explained that they did not have summer jobs. He advised me to go to the editorial department on the fifth floor where they were sometimes looking for copy boys. That sounded good to me, and it was back to the elevator.

The elevator opened directly into a small office, and a young guy listened to my plea for employment. "You want to talk to Sterling Riley," he counseled and went off in search of Mr. Riley. After a brief wait, a middle-aged man approached and told me he was Sterling Riley. "What the hell do you want?" he demanded in the most threatening voice I had encountered since beginning my summer job search. Riley was less threatening when I haltingly explained that I was looking for a summer job. "When can you start?" he asked. I told him I would not finish my sophomore year for five more weeks but was available Saturdays and Sundays or after school right away. "Stick your books and your jacket there," he ordered, pointing to a shelf in the small front office, "and follow me."

Riley led me to a long horseshoe-shaped desk where eight or ten men were working. An older gentleman sat at the head of the desk, apparently in charge. "This is the copy desk," Riley explained, "and when this copy editor hands you a piece of copy, you put it in one of these"—he pointed to several pneumatic tubes—"and shoot it up to the composing room." With that, he turned on his heel and walked away. Although I did not realize it at the time, I now had a job—and in the newspaper business. What a start!

I spent the rest of the afternoon sending copy to the composing room until the copy desk closed down, sometime before six. The office emptied out in a hurry. Riley came over during the course of the afternoon and asked whether I would be back the next day at the same time. When I told him I would, he added that the staff worked all night Saturday but not on Sunday. As I explained all this to the rest of the family when I got home, "That means I can still caddy on Sunday . . . after church, of course," I added, to the delight of my beaming mother. "How much are they paying you?" my older sister, Mary, asked. I sheepishly answered that I had no idea. It turned out I made $12 a week for a full week of work, $2.40 per day. That $12 wage resulted in a take-home pay of $11.88, with the 12 cents going to Social Security.

{ 13

My parents never took anything out of those early earnings. Friday was payday, and when I went home with my paycheck, my mother advised that I put it away toward tuition. She warned, "You'll be going to college in two years and you better start preparing for that."

Let me make things clear: Our family was never poor. At least, nobody told us we were poor or referred to us as poor. My father, and later my mother, had emigrated from Ireland with scant education but with a firm desire to find work in what they referred to as "this new world." We lived in a neat row house in a decent northeast Baltimore neighborhood. I was born John Francis Cashen in 1925, in my parents' upstairs front bedroom, and joined two older sisters, Mary and Nora. Their first little brother, Cornelius, had died from a ruptured appendix before he was two years old, and before I was born. When I was two, my younger brother, Neil, appeared, making it two boys and two girls.

Much later, I realized that being voted into a Hall of Fame—anybody's hall of fame—always seemed to remind me to go back to my roots, to examine where I came from. I was lucky to be so honored a handful of times, having been elected to the Halls of Fame of the Baltimore Orioles, the New York Mets, the state of Maryland, and Loyola University of Maryland. Each time brought memories of my mother and father, immigrants from Tipperary, Ireland, with little education but with a burning determination that their fate would not be shared by their four U.S.-born off-spring. This is a great country, a message they breathed almost daily, but you must get an education. My father not only preached that philosophy, he lived it.

Cornelius Joseph Cashen, my father, known in the business world as C.J. and to his family and friends as Con or Connie, came to this country as a young man in 1912, with what he described as a fourth-grade education. He landed in Baltimore, and soon after he got settled, he decided it was time to marry a girl he was keen on, Brigid Mary Ryan, from his home county of Tipperary. She was then working as a domestic in Lowell, Massachusetts. Con accomplished that mission quickly, then got a steady job scrub-bing floors at Baltimore's Fleischmann yeast plant. The job was as high as he could expect to go as an immigrant with a fourth-grade education, he told me. So he started befriending the firemen and engineers at the plant, who were unstinting in offering helpful advice. They steered him to night school, where he spent long nights over many years to earn a stationary engineer degree.

I have always remained incredibly proud of both my parents. An article written by the head of the Fleischmann plant is great testimony to why I so respected my father. L. H. Windholz paid tribute to Con Cashen in the following piece for the company bulletin, nearly a century ago:

By keeping eternally at it [his job] during the day, and studying every book on mechanics and engineering, he [Connie] could get hold of at night, he finally achieved his ambition of a first grade engineers' license. As a result of his persistence, pluck and perseverance, when the big new plant of the Fleischmann Company was built, and the question of a chief engineer came up, there was no one else thought of or considered but 'Connie,' the man who had won his spurs by hard work and keeping at it, who had never lost sight of the goal he had set for himself just a short eight years before.

When a fellow gets discouraged and is inclined to say to himself, "There isn't the opportunity nowadays for a fellow that there used to be," why just let him stop for a moment and consider the case of Cornelius Cashen, Chief Engineer Extraordinary.

When the yeast plant later closed, Con was out of work for a short time, which was a completely new experience for him. He eventually hooked up with the Baltimore Public School System { 15 and was placed in charge of the heating plants in a section of the city. There was no such thing as air conditioning in the system at this time. Equipped with his hard-earned stationary engineer degree, Con gradually was given more responsibility and retired years later as the supervising engineer for the whole Baltimore School System, with more than four hundred employees reporting to him.

My father never let up on his sermon about getting an education, and his words never fell on deaf ears in the Cashen household. And when Con was home, family evenings often were brightened by his fiddle playing, a talent he had brought from the Old Sod.

So the Cashen family never missed a meal, Sunday Mass, or the necessary school clothes, although to accomplish such worthy goals, Con did engage in a small subterfuge from time to time. Having gotten a late start on his professional career, Con had to constantly persuade his employers that he was younger than their records showed. So he would put a five-dollar bill in an envelope, send it to a parish back in Ireland, and request a baptismal certificate that showed him to be years younger than their current records. I never knew how he pulled this off, but I do know he did it several times. The reason I have knowledge of this devious activity is that a short time after he had retired, my dad called me in a panic and told me that the government had notified him they wanted to question him about the validity of his retirement.

The federal government had set a date, a time, and a location to meet with him. By then I had completed law school, passed the bar, and was a bona fide lawyer. My father asked if I would go with him to the meeting, and of course I agreed. The meeting was short and sweet. The government official said he had three and maybe four different dates for Con Cashen's birth. The purpose of the meeting was to validate one of the dates. "No doubt you are eligible for Social Security," the official promised, "it's just a matter of selecting one of these dates." Con picked one, and the whole proceeding took twelve minutes.

Each spring, my father headed to Sears Roebuck, as it was known in the 1940s, to buy paint and whatever else was needed to put the house in tiptop condition. As we grew, the row house seemed smaller and smaller, and we started looking for larger quarters. This led us to a spacious house on a large lot in Gardenville, in the north end of Baltimore. The same dedication to upkeep, perhaps more, followed. The yard included a small but flourishing grape arbor, and wine making was the obvious result. Allowed to taste only a thimbleful of the finished product, I could not testify as to the caliber of the wine, but it got rave notices from those old enough to partake.

Like the taste of good wine, memories of my parents and growing up in Baltimore are sweet. I could not then have imagined a career in baseball or any of my other career pursuits.

16 }

Shocking Developments

A few days after taking over my new assignment, the Orioles' front office had a major shock. Lee MacPhail announced he had been offered, and had accepted, an interesting and challenging new baseball job as assistant to the new commissioner of baseball, retired general William Eckert, who was appointed after Ford Frick's retirement. Lee would be leaving the Orioles and moving back to New York, where his father, the ubiquitous Larry MacPhail, had gleaned countless headlines while heading the Yankees. Lee already was well known around the Big Apple and his return was a great move for baseball. Responding quickly to MacPhail's departure, Hoffberger made it clear that I, Frank Cashen, would take over as the chief operating officer and put together the appropriate staff.

Right from the start, Hoffberger told me I was expected to be the one to answer all the questions. "I don't want to be talking to staff people to find out what I need to know," he lectured. "You talk to them, and just keep me informed." I remembered his warning and made sure he never learned anything important by first reading it in the newspaper or hearing it on radio or TV.

Lee MacPhail was, to my way of thinking, the best baseball man in the business, and I said so publicly. He had gathered a lot of good young talent in the field—even before the blockbuster trade we were about to make.

After serving in the commissioner's office, MacPhail went back to the New York Yankees (where he had been farm director and player personnel director in the 1950s). He was general manager of the pinstripers from 1967 to 1973, then served ten years as American League president. During that time, Lee was embroiled in the famous "pine tar incident" in a disputed game between the Yankees and the Kansas City Royals in 1983. As junior circuit president, MacPhail upheld Kansas City's protest, restoring a home run by the Royals' George Brett. The Royals slugger had had a game-winning homer taken away by the home plate umpire after the Yankees argued that Brett's bat had pine tar extending too far up the barrel of the bat, a rule violation.

I was later present at the owners' meeting when Lee was enthusiastically nominated to run for the job of baseball commissioner when that vacancy occurred in the 1970s. To my dismay, he promptly declined the offer, and Bowie Kuhn, from the law firm that represented the National League at that time, took over the post—and Major League Baseball moved on. Lee's only excuse for declining the offer was that he just wasn't interested in the job.

Television and its big-money offers were getting involved with the game, and soon things changed in innumerable ways. While there had been indicators of tv's potential, few of us, including me, foresaw that it would become the major factor in the financial future of the big league game.

Lee was the middle generation of a prominent baseball family. His father, Larry, was a top executive with the Yankees as well as the Cincinnati Reds and the Brooklyn Dodgers. At the time of his death in 2012, Lee MacPhail was the oldest living member of the National Baseball Hall of Fame. Lee's son, Andy, was recently president of the Orioles. A fourth-generation MacPhail, Lee IV, was a scouting director with the O's.

As he departed the Orioles in 1966, Lee also left us a log of office talent. Among them were Joe Hamper, Harry Dalton, Lou Gorman, Jerry Sachs, and Bob Brown. Jack Dunn III, whose family had owned the Orioles before they were introduced into the Majors in 1954, had been an assistant to Lee and had baseball knowledge aplenty. Dunn was valuable in his position, but I did not see him as a future "head guy." Hoffberger eventually agreed and went along with my other thoughts on personnel, largely gleaned from what I had observed the previous season.

Hamper would remain as comptroller. Gorman got a nudge further up the ladder in the operations department. Brown would still be the traveling secretary, a key job that involves facilitating the movement of the team around the country. Sachs advised me that he was leaving to accept another job.

I selected Harry Dalton, who had successfully worked his way through the lower echelons of the O's baseball system, to be vice president of baseball operations and, in many ways, my number one assistant. At this stage, I didn't name a general manager, as I realized that a lot of those duties were going to fall my way. GMS in those days were the chief operating officers (COOS) of the clubs and in charge of everything: radio and television, the stadium, the playing field, the Minor Leagues, ticket sales, public relations, club publications, spring training, and, of course, the Major League club. All of the above fell squarely on the shoulders of the general manager. Well, not quite squarely. There were well-qualified individuals who labored in those departments, but they all answered to the GM. Contrary to what was later written, Dalton was never GM. He remained VP of baseball operations, a role in which he was unusually good.

{ 19

The kind of GM just described was a dinosaur in baseball lore, and soon extinct. Within a very few years, the GM was assigned only to the playing phase of the game—for the most part running the Major League club. Some GMS did handle the scouts and Minor League clubs; others, the big league entry only. Some, like Harry Dalton, who seven years later moved to the California Angels as an old-time GM, quickly found out that he had no interest in performing the ancillary duties and later moved to the Milwaukee Brewers, where he restricted himself only to the player phase of the game. Gorman, who journeyed to Kansas City and then to

Seattle, made the same move. John Schuerholz, who originally
started with the Orioles, did likewise and ultimately was the general manager and subsequently president of the Atlanta Braves,
where he enjoyed a long and very successful career. Schuerholz
came from a very athletic Baltimore-area family, heavy in soccer players. He was a junior high school teacher at the time, and
Hoffberger had met with him and passed him along to me with
the thought that I might find him useful. I was impressed with
John, who, among other things, had played college baseball and
soccer at nearby Towson State. Having no front office openings
at that time, I nonetheless opened a slot in the Minor League department, and John became an assistant in the farm and scouting
departments under Gorman. It proved to be a successful coupling.
I was not totally surprised, a couple years later, when Gorman
moved up to the general manager position with the Royals and
asked permission to take Schuerholz with him as farm director.

I hired Gorman back as assistant GM when I was with the New
York Mets in the 1980s. Later he moved on to the Boston Red
Sox, a team he had rooted for since childhood, where he did a
fabulous job as GM.

I knew we had a very special talent pool in our off-the-field
Orioles staff, so it was not surprising that Dalton, Gorman, and
Schuerholz all went on to be outstanding general managers with
other clubs. Each built teams that got to the World Series during
their tenures.

One challenge facing the Orioles was trying to compete with
the Baltimore Colts. Early on in my tenure we lost Jerry Sachs,
a good public relations director who was only getting better. He
was young and personable. When I asked why he was leaving, he
said that there was nothing he had done or could do to change
the public's high esteem for the Baltimore Colts football team
and virtual disregard for the Orioles. At the time, the Colts were
consistent contenders in the National Football League and the
darlings of the local media. It was difficult to argue the point with

this bright, young professional, who then headed to Atlanta to work for Coca-Cola.

While the Colts preceded the Orioles in Baltimore by a couple of years, their success on the gridiron in the late 1950s vaulted them into first place among local sports preferences and enthusiasm. Led by quarterback Johnny Unitas, the Colts thrilled Baltimore with back-to-back NFL titles in 1958 and 1959. Who can forget Alan Ameche's one-yard plunge to beat the New York Giants in the '58 championship game, the first to be nationally televised and later called "The Greatest Game Ever Played"?

By contrast, the Orioles were slow out of the starting gate in Baltimore. They were once the lowly St. Louis Browns, noted for perennial last-place finishes and sparse attendance in a city that loved the high-flying baseball Cardinals. Baseball owners approved the Browns' move to Baltimore for the start of the 1954 season. Despite the enthusiastic welcome by Baltimore fans (they drew {21} over a million the first year), the team's on-field performance lagged for most of the 1950s until Lee MacPhail came on the scene in 1958 as general manager and later president. Despite some solid teams and some runs at the pennant in the early 1960s, the O's had not yet made it to a World Series as we prepared for the 1966 season.

Soon after joining the Orioles, I called a staff meeting and explained to the group that I had no certain answer to the Colts' popularity and the Orioles' lack of same. I said we had to seize every opportunity to preach the gospel of Oriole baseball to any group, large or small, and through all media, and something good would happen. Fortunately, we had a bunch of good speakers. Dunn, Dalton, and Gorman were great on their feet. Also, a young man we had hired to help with marketing, Bud Freeman, may have been the best of them all. Then too, I had never met a microphone I didn't like. Any time there was a group of five or more who needed a speaker, the Orioles were quick to provide one.

Then the Colts did us what I considered to be a major favor. Don Kellet, the team's coo, had built a formidable organization and was especially skilled at public relations. Suddenly, Carroll Rosenbloom, the owner of the team, inexplicably fired Kellet. No plausible reason was given for that grossly unpopular move. I always felt that Rosenbloom was jealous of Kellet and all the plaudits he received, and wanted those accolades for himself. For whatever reason, the Colts were never afterward as formidable off the field as on, and our little band of orators was making good progress. The Orioles' sweep of the LA Dodgers the following fall also brought us a lot more local interest, to say the least.

And speaking of raising the Orioles' image, history accepts that Hoffberger first sent me to the club to be vp of marketing, a position that I fully understood after working at National Brewing for four years. Coming with that assignment was a flood of ideas. "How can you change the opinion and impression the average fan had of the Orioles?"

One of my very first thoughts was that the Oriole "bird" that was pictured on the front of the official baseball cap, and served as the club's symbol, was too sedentary. It was supposed to be a small oriole, but it looked to me more like a tiny sparrow. Having just concluded a series of new beer commercials at National, the bulk of them being cartoon related, I had a couple ideas that I wanted to discuss with the Los Angeles advertising crowd. I contacted Stan Walsh, who had done some work for National Brewing. Stan had been a cartoonist for the Walt Disney Studio prior to opting for commercial work, and we had been fairly good friends. In short order Stan sent me examples of aggressive cartoon birds, one of which became the new symbol of the Orioles and was immediately transferred to the 1966 baseball caps.

The cartoon bird was a fixture during the ten years I was running the organization, which turned out to be the most successful in team history. It stayed atop the cap till 1989, when new owner Peter Angelos decided to go back to the cute little original bird.

However, the return of the sparrow-like bird did little to improve the fortunes of the team over the next twenty-some years. In 2012 the old cartoon bird version was brought back to the caps and, amazingly, the Orioles had their first winning season in fourteen years.

That first season, I felt the team was in good shape. We had veteran Hank Bauer, the former star New York Yankees outfielder, as manager, as well as a lengthy list of good young starting pitchers, a solid experienced bullpen, and an infield anchored by Brooks Robinson at third base and Boog Powell at first. Perhaps we needed one more hitter. That's what my notes said.

5

Parting Gift

Events moved swiftly after that in the fall of 1965. Lee MacPhail had another surprise to share with us. He had been working quietly with the Cincinnati Reds on a possible trade. The essence of the deal was that the Orioles would send veteran pitcher Milt Pappas to the Reds for outfielder Frank Robinson, a former MVP in the National League. There were fringe players included on both sides but, basically, Pappas and Robinson were the big pieces. The Reds had already agreed to the trade, and Lee had asked for a little more time to run it by the new owners in Baltimore. Lee told us that it was up to us. A yes or no answer to Cincinnati was already overdue. I decided to talk to my new staff and get their thoughts.

We had brought manager Hank Bauer to Baltimore to meet the new owner, so he was readily available. I talked to him privately and Bauer said his recommendation would be to not make the trade. (His thinking, at the time, was reasonable. However, in later years when the wisdom of the swap was undeniable, he insisted that he was always in favor of adding Robinson.) Bauer's negative vote was solid and for the following reasons: He felt he had a good ball club, good enough to win, or at least to be a strong contender, and he didn't want to upset the chemistry; the trade would cost him "my best pitcher, Milt Pappas, and pitchers of that stripe are impossible to replace"; and Robinson had been a bad actor. Bringing that kind of individual into the clubhouse doesn't make sense, Bauer noted. (But let me be quick to point out

that throughout his career in Baltimore, Frank Robinson never
caused a single problem, on or off the field.)

All this seemed to make sense to me. I remember my initial
feeling was to agree with Bauer. He was certainly prepared for my
questions. Next, I asked Dalton to tell me how our other baseball
people felt about the deal. Within a few hours, Dalton was back
and reported that he and the rest of his group unanimously felt we
should make the trade. Posing the question to Jack Dunn proved
no help. He was "on the fence." He could see some advantages
and some disadvantages, which by this time pretty well described
my own feelings.

Lastly, I asked the departing MacPhail for his thoughts. He
declined to take a position, maintaining that he hadn't made a
final decision. I certainly understood his reluctance to get in the
middle of the debate. But I felt he wouldn't have spent so much
time working on the deal if he didn't consider it a good move
for the O's. Speaking with Hoffberger in a face-to-face meeting
the next day, I explained the Frank Robinson dilemma. I added,
"We've got a problem." I'll never forget his response: "What do
you mean we've got a problem; you're running the club now. It's
your decision!"

It was now December 1965; spring training was only eight
weeks away and the clock was ticking. I had been warned that
our answer to the Reds was already past due. Juggling the opposing arguments in my own mind, I did what I had frequently
done before and after. I took a large yellow legal pad and drew
a line down the middle and scratched out the two sides of the
argument.

Logically, I felt the manager had made the stronger case. However, after paying particular attention to the team of the previous
year, I did not agree that Milt Pappas was the club's best starting
pitcher. That honor belonged to Steve Barber and some younger
studs, like Jim Palmer, Dave McNally, and Wally Bunker. With this
in mind, I decided to make the Robinson trade. (That judgment

{ 25

on pitching was vindicated when these three pitchers would star in the 1966 Series sweep of the O's over the Dodgers.) After serious reflection, I had also concluded that Frank Robinson could well be the featured player in a new marketing campaign. I told Hoffberger of my decision, called in Dalton, and instructed him to contact the Reds and clean up the details.

We flew Robby (as Robinson was then known) to Baltimore in December 1965 for a press conference and had dinner with him the night before at the Owl Bar in the Belvedere Hotel. Bob Brown (then the traveling secretary), Dalton, and I were the hosts. Robinson came by himself, and as expected, he was relatively stoic throughout. The one exception was when we explained that all of our players were treated the same. Whether your name is Boog Powell, Brooks Robinson, Paul Blair, or Frank Robinson, the same player rules apply. "I accept that, if you say so," he replied. "But," his eyes narrowed as he continued, "if I find out you're lying to me . . ." and his voice trailed off without finishing the sentence. Other than that, the dinner was civil. He spoke quietly and confidently, made no negative comments about the Reds, but indirectly seemed to be searching for reasons why they traded him.

The rest, of course, is history. Robby had one of the greatest individual seasons in baseball that first season with us, winning the coveted Triple Crown with a .316 batting average, 49 home runs, and 122 RBIS and leading us to a World Series title over the Dodgers. Frank Robinson played for the O's for another four years, until 1971, and was a key performer during that time. However, as I frequently remind myself, MacPhail was the instigator of the deal. And, as it turned out, the initial move to get Robinson was a pretty nice legacy for him to leave to Baltimore. I made plenty of Major League trades during my years in baseball, but that one, my very first, was the most agonizing.

Brooks Robinson, our veteran third baseman, often explained the club's performance by saying, "We had a good ball club, but Frank Robinson taught us how to win."

The '66 Orioles easily won the AL pennant, finishing with a record of 97-63, nine games ahead of the second-place Minnesota Twins. In addition to Frank Robinson's incredible year, first baseman Boog Powell delivered 34 home runs and 109 RBIS, while Brooks Robinson hit 23 round-trippers with 100 RBIS. Led by pitching stalwarts Dave McNally, 13-6, and Jim Palmer, 15-10, the Orioles never looked back and breezed to the AL title and the chance to face the NL champion Los Angeles Dodgers in the Fall Classic.

Four Straight

That 1966 World Series did not go as most fans and experts had expected. The baseball world was stunned by our sweep of the potent Los Angeles Dodgers. Their team was loaded with talent, including Sandy Koufax and Don Drysdale, two of the best pitchers in baseball. Ironically, the last World Series sweep had occurred three years earlier when the Dodgers, behind MVP Sandy Koufax,

took four straight from the New York Yankees. World Series sweeps had occurred only three other times since the 1930s.

The 1966 World Series produced more than one oddity. It was the first time a club had used only four pitchers in the series. Dave McNally started the opener against the Dodgers' Don Drysdale. After a shaky start, McNally was removed in the third inning with the lead. Moe Dobrowski, selected from the Chicago Cubs in an off-season draft, took over and kept the LA club silent the rest of the way, for a 5–2 win. Jim Palmer got the assignment the next day and shut out the Dodgers, 6–0, defeating the legendary Sandy Koufax, in what proved to be the last game of his amazing career.

Those first two games were played in Los Angeles and were followed by a joyous but jarring flight home. Halfway across the country, the plane suddenly dropped a thousand feet, sending food and drink up on the ceiling of the plane. A few passengers, who had been standing in the aisles, followed the food to the top. Incredibly, there were no serious injuries. An off day followed and a giant billboard near Baltimore's Memorial Stadium proclaimed, "Would You Believe, Four Straight."

Pitcher Wally Bunker, an early O's bonus baby, stepped into Game Three—the first World Series game ever played in Baltimore—and beat the Dodgers, 1–0. In many ways, of the four, this third was the most surprising game. Three wins, and possibly it could all be over the next day. McNally was going against Drysdale again, and a thought that had been creeping foggily into my mind suddenly became clear. If we won, there had to be a big party that night and we, understandably, had made no preparations.

Searching for an idea, I reached back to an old friend, Mike Costanza. He was one of the owners and operators of the Tail of the Fox, a private club on York Road, north of Towson, in Baltimore County. Mike was a very swift and dependable center fielder on my old fast-pitch softball team. I knew he would have to shut his shop down to his members, but the town would be crazy over its first world championship whether in four straight or even if it took five games. No persuasion was necessary. Mike readily {29 agreed but cautioned that he hoped we would give him at least two hours after the game was over to handle the preparations.

McNally did his part in Game Four as Drysdale and the Dodgers went down for the count in another 1–0 game. Not only had we swept the Dodgers, but O's pitchers allowed only two earned runs in the Series and shut out the Dodgers for a World Series record thirty-three consecutive innings—from the fourth inning of Game One to the end of Game Four. Frank Robinson, who hit two home runs off Drysdale in Game One and scored the winning run in Game Four, was voted Series MVP.

Clubhouse festivities behind them, the players changed to coats and ties, collected their wives or girlfriends, and headed to the Tail of the Fox. My lasting memory of the first-class celebration was seeing my wife, Jean, balancing herself on one leg, surrounded by two or three pitchers drinking champagne out of one of her satin slippers.

And speaking of Jean, it seems to me that there are a number of lotteries in life, and few have to do with financial prizes. The one that comes instantly to mind is marriage. And just as instantly comes the knowledge that in this sweepstake I won first prize. I simply can't say enough about Jean, who has been my partner since 1950. Way back in midcentury I was going out with numerous young ladies. The popular puzzle was when, and if, Frank was ever going to get married. I had a younger brother, Neil, two years behind me, age twenty-two. He had his own circle of friends, including a string of comely young ladies, all of whom were several years younger than me.

One day I told him that I was looking for a new young female friend and was going to give a particular one of those young ladies a call to see if she was interested in a date. He was quick to respond with the following caution: "I wouldn't call her. She is pretty but doesn't have much personality. Why don't you call Jean Altman? She is more your type. I think she is great-looking and has a great personality." I hadn't met Jean, but I recognized her as a tall, lanky blond and was told she was a good athlete.

"She's too tall for me," I protested, "and she probably wouldn't want to go out with me." I half remembered that Jean was the goalie on the Baltimore City female ice hockey team and that I had seen an impressive picture of her in the *Evening Sun* newspaper. "If she's too tall," my brother shot back, "it's not going to bother Jean. She's got too much confidence to let a little thing like that bother her." It was the first and last time I ever had to introduce myself to a young lady as Neil Cashen's older brother.

We went to a dance at the local Arundel Boat Club on our first date and I found her to be an excellent dancer as well as, to my eyes, the best-looking lady in the place. We hit it off immediately, as she told me, among other things, that her mother had been voted Miss Arundel Boat Club a lot of years before. When I first rang her doorbell, I learned that her father was a lieutenant in the Baltimore Police Department. Not bad for parents, I thought—a police lieutenant and a beauty queen.

Jean and I went at it hot and heavy for quite a few months until I finally broke down and asked her to marry me. She consented and we agreed to arrange a wedding quietly and quickly to avoid a host of practical problems, mostly related to the ceremony. Time, as it usually does, eventually solved these difficulties.

Soon began a steady stream of welcome children. Gregory came first and was followed by Terry, Tim, Brian, Sean, and then two girls, Stacey and Blaise. Jean managed all of this exceedingly well, and in the years that followed did an even more wondrous job, as their father wandered through several jobs only to end up in baseball, where he spent his days and frequently his nights watching grown men, in knickered uniforms, play little-boy games across the length and breadth of the country. Meanwhile, she— and she alone—drove to and from a variety of schools, Little League baseball games, and lacrosse practices. In addition, Jean helped with seven forms of homework assignments and provided escorts to church, all while her husband was obstinately "working." You can easily figure out who was the most valuable player in our household.

After the Sweep

After the excitement of the 1966 World Series sweep had subsided, my thoughts turned to the winter work ahead. Frank Robinson, Brooks Robinson, Boog Powell, Dave Johnson, Paul Blair, as well as those aforementioned standout pitchers, Palmer et al., had to be signed for the following season, and still the final payroll figure was shy of $1 million. This was a few years before collective bargaining, and how times have changed.

If head baseball guys are allowed to have favorites, Jim Palmer was always one of mine. Several weeks before the World Series victory, Jim dropped by my office. By way of starting the conversation, he blurted, "Mr. Cashen, I tried to do what you said but I couldn't because I'm not old enough." I was caught by surprise, and I asked him what he was talking about.

"You told the whole team that if we were looking for someplace to live, to buy a house in Baltimore. You pointed out how leftover cash from the MLB's generous meal and living expenses allowance would pretty much cover mortgage payments half of the year and there would be opportunities to get jobs here in the off-season." And, he added, "I thought that if we win the World Series, the extra cash could be a down payment. Susie and I have tried several places, but neither of us is twenty-one and that means we can't sign a legal contract."

"Don't worry about it," I replied, trying to hide my surprise. "I can take care of that." It only took a phone call to a local finance company, in which the Hoffbergers had an interest. It helped that the manager was a personal friend of mine and that I agreed to co-sign for the loan. Jim was married to his high school love, Susie Ryan, who had to lead Scottsdale, Arizona, in good looks. Having watched Jimmy through his full first season in the Majors, I was assured that he was going to make plenty of money in the future. Cosigning his mortgage was hardly a gamble.

Even before the 1966 season had started, I had been occupied with filling the hole in my front office staff that Jerry Sachs's departure had left. The public relations job was a tricky one to fill. We were looking for someone skilled in media work as well as able to handle the general public. The media part was expanding. In the past the job involved working with a few local newspaper writers, but after we won, it involved a lot of national radio and television people who were taking up more and more time.

Somewhere in my previous travels I had come upon Joe Mc-Bride, a Notre Dame alumnus, who was then working at *Life* { 33 magazine. He seemed to me to be just the candidate for the job. He agreed and spent that successful 1966 season learning the ropes. A devoted cigar smoker, Joe did an excellent job with the out-front part of the business, but he was lax in the inside portion of his duties. He was good at talking about the club and verbally sparring with the media bunch and he was more than adequate in another part of his chores—dealing with the players. Despite all this, the eagerly awaited team press guide, setting up the 1967 season, was embarrassingly late, and the media part of the business seemed to fall behind in other ways as well. As it turned out, the '67 season was embarrassing in all ways. The O's, the defending champions, finished sixth, fifteen and a half games behind the AL champion Boston Red Sox. At this point, after just one season, Joe McBride opted for other challenges and left us.

We moved on, and going into the following season, I made one of the best trades of my baseball career. We moved Bob Brown from traveling secretary to head of public relations and switched Phil Itzoe, formerly deep in the public relations department, to traveling secretary, a spot in which he excelled for forty-one years, the longest tenure of anyone in that position in professional sports. Bob Brown brought new enthusiasm to the PR department and introduced a new twist. He dove into his book of statistics and came up with figures that showed what the current roster hit against opposing pitchers and, conversely, what our pitchers did against opposition batters. Of course, he passed along this valuable information to the manager. Believe it or not, Brown worked this all out with pencil and paper. When computers became available, the whole database moved there. All Major League clubs now utilize some form of Brown's formula.

In fact, the whole national pastime makes extensive use of information technology. Simple scouting reports on free agent prospects are submitted to the parent club via computer and become part of the club's permanent records. These records are quite extensive. For example, long after I retired, I reviewed early scouting reports on Cal Ripken Jr., the legendary Orioles infielder, and was amazed to see that he was being followed as a pitcher and a hitter while he was still in high school. Ultimately, he was tapped to be an infielder in order to get his bat into the game every day.

Statistics were always a part of baseball but were given a huge shot in the arm when, in 1977, an unofficial baseball statistician, Bill James, started to publish a yearly treatise on the subject. Then came computers. Billy Beane, one of my early draft choices for the New York Mets in 1980, had become general manager of the Oakland Athletics in 1998, when an Ivy League computer whiz talked Beane into using the analytical principles as an aid in scrutinizing the abilities of ballplayers, particularly young ones who were overlooked or undervalued. Beane later became famous as the subject of Michael Lewis's book *Moneyball* (and the 2011 feature film), but his surge to general managership was fast, triggered by a keen baseball mind. When his uneventful playing career seemed to be ending in the A's Minor League system, he asked for a job as an advance baseball scout, and his rise up the front office began in short order. He believes, as I do, that you build a successful team from the bottom up and that there is no substitute for good scouting.

The post-championship year of 1967 was a disappointment. When things didn't seem to improve early in 1968, we began talking seriously about making changes. By the end of the 1967 season, I remember that our first baseman, Boog Powell, already a large man, had put on a lot of extra weight. At the end of the season, we had a personal, man-to-man talk. I explained that his ever-increasing weight had begun to affect his game and that he needed to do something about it. Powell vehemently disagreed. "There is nothing wrong with my weight," Boog proclaimed. "I'm a big guy and I can carry the pounds." As I recall, I offered a contract that called for a certain amount of money and an additional bonus if he reported to spring training considerably lighter. A disgruntled Booger left Baltimore for his winter home in Florida, insisting that we were terribly unreasonable.

{ 35

Powell lived in South Florida, not far from our spring-training base in Miami. Word came back to me that Boog was making little or no progress in the battle with his belly. He seemed to be eating and drinking as much as ever. Through Christmas and the New Year, he was never one for working out, and that year was no exception. But then, with only a few weeks remaining until spring training, I heard that he was working furiously to lose weight, including not eating any substantial food. Down to the week before spring training, reports had it that Mr. Powell was still eight or ten pounds over the agreed weight. He answered that challenge by not eating at all. Diet sodas and occasional scraps of low-calorie food were all he took in that final week.

Somehow the press got wind of the story, and Powell's first appearance in spring training was eagerly awaited. Knowing this was going to be the case, Boog showed up well before the usual starting time. He looked awful, not having eaten a decent meal in six weeks, but he tipped the Miami scales with a pound to spare. He'd won his battle and immediately noted that he was entitled to full salary, including his bonus! Booger loved food but he loved money, too. After going to the batting cage and hitting nothing but weak ground balls, Booger made another announcement. "I can't play at this weight," he declared. "I'm too light. I've got no power." It was fruitless to explain to Powell that by using the four-month period between the close of one season and the start of spring training to exercise and diet, his extra pounds would come off and stay off. He didn't want to hear it. He started to load up on food that afternoon, and before the start of the season he was back up to 260.

While his performance in 1968 was not his best, the Booger came back the next two years with great numbers—.304 BA and 37 home runs in 1969 and a .297 BA and 35 homers in 1970. Boog was MVP that year and played a giant role in the Orioles' winning 108 games and running away with the AL East. In spite of the weight problems, Powell was a nifty guy. He was great with his teammates and adored by Baltimore fans. He was a solid contributor to that string of great Oriole clubs. As a sidebar, I should add that eating continued to be a subject never far from Boog's heart. In fact, after he retired, he started a fast food stand called Boog's Barbecue, operated inside Camden Yards. It is run by Boog's son, "Little Boog," and has a second location on the boardwalk at Ocean City, Maryland. "Big Boog" is a constant presence, signing autographs for appreciative, hungry fans while still giving a lot of attention to the barbecue business.

We finished that post-championship year of 1967 in sixth place, fifteen and a half games behind the pennant-winning Red Sox. Clearly, we faced a tough road to recovery the following year.

Earl of Baltimore

In midseason of 1968, we fired manager Hank Bauer and replaced him with Earl Weaver, a Minor League manager out of our system who had joined the O's coaching staff at the start of the season. From the start this move was popular with our organization, since Weaver had compiled an impressive record managing the Oriole farm teams for nearly a decade. Thus began Weaver's long, successful run as the O's manager, from midseason 1968 through 1982 and again in 1985 and '86. During his tenure, Weaver's teams won six Eastern Division titles, four league pennants, and a World Series championship. He had only one losing year, 1986, and his teams had five seasons with one hundred or more victories. Weaver had returned from retirement in 1985 and retired again after the 1986 season. Never fired; twice retired.

Earl Sidney Weaver, the little man with the Napoleon complex, had a sign on the wall of his office that read "It's what you learn after you think you know everything that counts." I puzzled over that sign for years and changed my mind about it as often as I changed it about some rookie ballplayers. In a lot of ways it is about Earl Sidney. Truly, though, the Sidney never fit the man who was simply Earl Weaver, who was, and let me say this emphatically, the best-ever Major League manager in baseball. The best? Yes, absolutely the best. Why? In short—and that is an apt description of Earl—because he was a manager for all seasons.

There are some managers who are good with a young ball club and some who are great with an experienced ball club. However, they are seldom, if ever, talented with both. Then there are some who do well with a mediocre team—one that finishes comfortably in the middle of the pack; not the best but not the worst. The bulk of skippers are in this last-mentioned category. There are also good Minor League leaders who never make it in the big show. Earl Weaver could simply do it all. Lord knows he could handle a pennant-bound club. He proved that time after time. But he could also take a bad club and make it better. And having come up as a manager through the Minor League system, he appreciated the lessons an individual player has to learn as he climbs the ladder to the big leagues.

Which brings me to one salient point that I felt was paramount in running a ball club: Players don't learn to win in the big leagues. They learn that in the Minors. For instance, in a crucial Minor League game, a potential double play ball is hit to the shortstop and he learns to handle it just as he will have to do three years later, perhaps in the World Series. The dominant thought in baseball seems to be that the Minors are simply for producing Major League players. To my mind, they are for providing *winning* Major League players, and I conducted my system to that end. Examples of this philosophy would be Dwight Gooden and Darryl Strawberry, who came to the Majors in different years, but neither played on a losing Minor League club throughout their journey to the Major Leagues.

Earl Weaver, though, never played in the Majors. He was signed to a professional contract by the St. Louis Cardinals as a seventeen-year-old infielder after graduating from Beaumont High School, just a few blocks from the Cardinals' home field, Sportsman's Park, in St. Louis. But after failing to climb that final rung of the ladder to the Majors, he seized the opportunity to manage in the Minors and won three championships there before joining the Orioles as first base coach in 1968, taking over as manager midseason.

My personal opinion that Earl was the best manager in the game didn't come while he was still managing for me in Baltimore, but after I had left for New York and had the opportunity to compare him with the National League skippers. It became clear to me that Weaver was in a class by himself. Earl frequently stated his philosophy about winning ball games as "pitching, defense, and three-run homers."

Earl was famous—better said, infamous—for his relations with umpires. Every year in spring training, at least so far as I knew, he carefully reread the official rule book. He could recite the rules by number and page and he did so whenever he had the opportunity to do so, much to the dismay of the umpires. He became a target for expulsion—a target that the umps would talk about among themselves in what they thought were private conversations. But bartenders and waitresses are prone to repeat what they have overheard from customers who let their guard down. And their tales were numerous.

That little guy who wore No. 4 on his uniform his entire Major League career was known to drink a little. Make that, was known to drink a lot. There was beer in the clubhouse after a game, but as soon as he could get to a real bar, hotel or otherwise, it was a G&T—a gin and tonic. As soon as the bartender put the first drink down on the bar, Earl would demand another. He always wanted to have that second one waiting before he had a gulp of the first.

His retorts to some of the inevitable questions were legendary. Asked why he wouldn't give another chance to a starting pitcher who had fallen from grace, he explained, "I've already given him more chances than I gave my first wife."

One of his outfielders, Pat Kelly, arrived in the clubhouse one Sunday morning in his usual happy mood and Weaver was probably nursing a hangover. "What are you so happy about?" No. 4 asked.

Kelly replied proudly, "I walk with the Lord."

"Why the hell don't you walk with the bases loaded?" was Earl's sour response.

For all of his managerial success and heroics, Weaver still had the little man complex. When he went to the pitching mound for any reason, the players who joined him there, including the pitcher, were cautious not to stand at the top of the mound but to go to level ground. As Earl went to the top spot, with his five-foot-seven-inch frame, he was better able to look them squarely in the eye. Weaver and pitching ace Jim Palmer had an ongoing dispute about this practice, but that was not their only one. Their differences, some serious and some foolish, lasted through the rest of their Major League careers.

Besides drinking and the rules of baseball, Earl Weaver had one other passionate interest, which was popular music. He had a photographic memory for song titles and lyrics, and it was not unusual for him to challenge the piano player in any bar to a contest: "I can name any song you can play." When the contest was over, and whether he won or not, Earl would insist on buying the musician a drink.

40 }   With Earl at the helm, the Birds were back in the pennant race in less than a year, winning the American League in 1969, and then, as I will describe, losing the World Series to the upstart New York Mets in an upset. I felt we had the best team in baseball, so that loss was a bitter one. While New York went crazy with the Miracle Mets, the 1969 series was a shocking disappointment to the Orioles, to Baltimore's legion of loyal fans, and to me.

Low Point to High Flyers

Our Orioles were heavily favored going into the 1969 World Series. We had Boog Powell, with 37 home runs and 121 RBIs; Frank Robinson, 32 homers and 100 RBIs; Brooks Robinson, 23 homers and 84 RBIs; and Paul Blair, 26 round-trippers and 76 RBIs. The Mets, a young franchise, were making their very first postseason appearance.

The O's took the first game, 4–1, in Baltimore's Memorial Stadium, beating twenty-five-game winner Tom Seaver behind the pitching of left-hander Mike Cuellar, who gave up only six hits and struck out eight. We thought we were on our way to another championship.

In Game Two, the Mets' Jerry Koosman pitched six hitless innings and, although the Orioles came back to tie the game in the seventh, the Mets put together a ninth-inning rally to win, 2–1. When the Series moved to Shea Stadium, the O's were shut out, 5–0, as Jim Palmer lost to Mets starter Gary Gentry, with relief help from a young Nolan Ryan. The Mets got a tremendous individual effort from their center fielder, Tommie Agee. Not only did Agee hit a first-inning homer off Palmer but he also made two spectacular, rally-killing catches.

Tom Seaver was on the mound in Game Four and took a 1–0 lead into the ninth inning. The O's rallied in the late innings, but the Mets' Ron Swoboda, who was born and raised in Baltimore, helped put down the rally with a diving, one-handed catch, one of his series of spectacular defensive plays. The Mets won it, 2–1, in the tenth, and unbelievably we were facing elimination the next day.

The O's seemed to regain their stride in Game Five as we took a 3–0 lead behind home runs by our pitcher, Dave McNally, and another by Frank Robinson. But the New Yorkers struck back when the Mets' Cleon Jones claimed he was hit on the foot by what became a controversial pitch. The umpires first ruled that he had not been hit, but Mets manager Gil Hodges argued that the ball showed a polish mark from Jones's shoe. This was after the ball had been in and out of the home team dugout. The umpire then reversed his call and awarded Jones first base. This was followed by Donn Clendenon's homer, and the Mets closed the gap to 3–2. The New Yorkers tied it in the sixth and took a 5–3 lead in the eighth. They held on to become the improbable World Champs and we went back to Baltimore with our tails between our legs. An exuberant Tom Seaver exclaimed, "God is living in New York City and he's a Mets fan."

Even in defeat, I continued to feel the O's had the better ball club. There were a lot of unexplainable incidents during the Series. There was a rumor that the umpires had secretly agreed "to get even" with Baltimore manager Earl Weaver, who had embarrassed several of the men in blue with his encyclopedic knowledge of the rules and consequent interpretation of same. Whether or not there was a plot afoot, they did get back at Weaver. Earl became the first manager in thirty-four years to be thrown out of a World Series game when, in the fourth game, he allegedly argued strikes and balls.

Another baffling incident cost the Orioles Game Four in extra innings. With the score tied in the Mets' half of the tenth inning, O's relief pitcher Pete Richert made what is recorded as a throwing error. The Mets had runners on first and second when pinch hitter C. J. Martin laid down a sacrifice bunt, but Richert hit Martin on the wrist with his attempted throw to first, allowing the winning run to score from second. Replays showed that

Martin was inside the first base line, which hindered Richert from making a good throw. (Interference calls are at the discretion of the umpires.) However, the Orioles did not protest the call and the Mets were up three games to one, needing only one more victory to win the Series.

Interestingly enough, I consider the 1969 Series—this unexpected loss to the New Yorkers—the absolute low point of my baseball career. And I feel that the 1986 World Series victory over the Boston Red Sox when I was with the Mets was the highlight of that same baseball life. Both high and low—seventeen years apart—took place in Shea Stadium. (That 1969 World Series was not the only bitter defeat for a Baltimore team at the hands of a New York club. In the football Super Bowl the previous January, Joe Namath's underdog Jets upset the heavily favored Baltimore Colts. Then the Baltimore Bullets basketball franchise lost out to the New York Knicks in the NBA championships the following year, which led the New York tabloids to dub Baltimore "Choke City.")

Earl Weaver's club was back in the thick of it in 1970, winning the AL title and then beating Cincinnati and its "Big Red Machine" in the World Series. Every World Series is memorable, and the O's battles with the Cincinnati Reds in 1970 and the Pittsburgh Pirates the following year were no exceptions.

You would be correct if you labeled the 1970 Series, in which the O's triumphed four games to one over the Big Red Machine, as the Brooks Robinson World Series. Baltimore's storied third baseman put on a defensive performance seldom, if ever, seen. The Cincinnati players referred to him as "Hoover," after the vacuum cleaner company. Brooks picked up everything that was even remotely hit in his direction. The Orioles—behind pitchers Jim Palmer, Tom Phoebus, and Dave McNally—won the first three games. After the O's dropped Game Four, Mike Cuellar came back to claim the championship. Brooks Robinson, who hit .426 in the five games, won an automobile as the World Series MVP. Johnny Bench, the Reds' captain and future Hall of Fame catcher, then quipped, "If we'd known that Brooks needed a car that bad, we would have bought him one."

Have no doubt, the most popular of that Oriole bunch was Brooks Robinson, a former second baseman converted to third baseman, where he performed beyond comprehension. A high school senior, drafted out of Little Rock, Arkansas, in 1955, he had polished his early baseball skills with an Oriole Minor League team in York, Pennsylvania, before joining the Birds. From the start, it was obvious that here was a special talent. He hit and threw right-handed but seemed to do everything else left-handed. When he ate, he used his left hand, he wrote left-handed, and generally he used the left side of his body for everything—everything else, that is, except baseball. Paul Richards, then general manager of the O's, directed the move that switched Robinson from second baseman to third, soon after coming to the team. From the start, he always excelled. No one debates that last claim; he excelled.

To my mind, Brooks did not have a superior arm when fielding a ground ball. You could not help but see his faultless footwork and the obvious speed he used to transfer the ball to his throwing position. In short, he unloaded so quickly you had to shake your head in disbelief, and he did so with compelling accuracy. He always got the ball over to first base in time. Basically a line-drive hitter, Robinson also could go long, hitting 268 home runs during his twenty-two-year span with the O's, the only Major League team for which he ever played. Not the fastest runner in the game, he was heady on the bases. In short, Brooks was the total package, offensively and defensively, and it added up to excellent. He was a man for the ages.

Robinson's baseball skills have been loudly proclaimed and the urge is to continue on that well-traveled path. But let me assure you that his profile as a human being is matched by, even surpasses, his baseball persona. He always had time for fans. He would sign autographs endlessly and chat with the kids and grownups alike for what seemed like forever. He was even depicted signing autographs in a famous picture by the legendary artist Norman Rockwell. When I took over the Orioles in 1966, I had box seats behind the dugout on the third base line at the old Memorial Stadium in Baltimore. We had a large and young family who had no interest in watching the game from the high perch of the press box. No, let them be down close to the battlefield where Brooks prevailed. That same Brooks, who kept my kids supplied with bubble gum and other goodies that came out of the Oriole dugout, also kept up a running dialogue while passing by the box between innings.

Brooks has been involved in a host of charitable activities for years, including Boy Scouting. With sixteen straight Gold Gloves and a lifetime 2,848 hits, Brooks was a first-ballot pick for baseball's Hall of Fame in 1983. Still beloved in Baltimore, Brooks was honored with a larger-than-life statue of his likeness that was unveiled in 2012 at Orioles Park at Camden Yards.   { 45

The 1970 World Series was notable for a number of reasons. It was the last Series in which all games were played in the afternoon. It was the first Series in Cincinnati's new Riverfront Stadium (Games One and Two), the first on artificial turf, and the first in which an African American, Emmett Ashford, was on the umpiring crew. Going into the Series, it looked to be a titanic struggle. The Big Red Machine had dominated the National League, finishing atop the NL West by fourteen and a half games and topping the Pittsburgh Pirates, three games to zip, in the NL championship game. We were not exactly slouches either, having won the AL East by fifteen games and sweeping the Minnesota Twins, 3–0, in the AL title series.

The Reds had a fearsome lineup with Johnny Bench, Tony Perez, Pete Rose, Bobby Tolan and Lee May among others. But we countered with three healthy twenty-game winners—Mike Cuellar, 24-8; Dave McNally, 24-9; and Jim Palmer, 20-10. Cuellar notched two of the four Oriole victories. McNally, who was the winning hurler in Game Three, also stunned the Reds with a grand slam home run during a 9–3 rout. After scuttling the Reds in 1970, we added San Diego Padres relief pitcher Pat Dobson to our staff. Pitching coach George Bamberger, another of our successful Minor League alumni, thought we should return Dobson to his old role as a starting pitcher. This done, the next year the Orioles had four twenty-game winners—Mike Cuellar, Pat Dobson, Dave McNally, and Jim Palmer.

That year, 1971, it was Baltimore versus Pittsburgh in the World Series, with the Pirates prevailing after what appeared to be an alley fight in which the best team won—but barely. The Orioles jumped out to a 2–0 lead in the Series, behind stellar pitching by McNally and Palmer, but the Pirates bounced back when they returned to their own ballpark and won the next three. Back in Baltimore, the O's behind McNally tied the Series at three each. But in Game Seven, Pirates pitcher Steve Blass went the full nine innings to lead his club to the championship. Pirates great Roberto Clemente hit .414 in the Series and was voted the most valuable player. For my money, that honor could well have gone to Blass, the surprising winner of two of the four games.

Clemente, an enormously gifted offensive and defensive outfielder from Puerto Rico, was an early leader of the Latino ballplayers who had started to migrate north to the Major Leagues, which previously had been almost exclusively played by United States citizens. First they came from Mexico, Cuba, and Puerto Rico, but soon they were joined by ballplayers from Venezuela, Nicaragua, Panama, and the Caribbean, most particularly, the Dominican Republic. Talented Latino ballplayers seemed to have arrived in droves and soon were a vital part of the sport. From Giants pitcher Juan Marichel in the 1970s to slugger Albert Pujols in this century, Latino players have enhanced the game with talent and heart. The increasing presence of Spanish-speaking players, as well as those from Japan and elsewhere, has added a language dimension to the job of manager. Not only do managers and coaches have to become versed in other tongues, but in some cases interpreters are needed. But few were more talented than Clemente, with a big powerful bat and rifle-like arm. After his tragic death in a plane crash in 1972, he was voted into the baseball Hall of Fame in Cooperstown.

Trying to examine the reasons for our defeat in the World Series, I kept coming back to one of my own axioms: Never let your whole ball club grow old together. Maybe that is not always popular with the fans, but you must regularly introduce new talent into the lineup. We had outfielder Don Baylor and shortstop Bobby Grich putting up eye-catching numbers for a couple of years in the Minors, and I had run out of excuses to keep sending them back to our Triple-A team.

I felt the time had come to part company with Frank Robinson, the hero of our 1966 championship year. I knew it was going to leave a lot of people hot under the collar, including a host of good baseball fans. Facing up to the move, I called in Robby and { 47 advised him of my thinking. I found him quite understanding and, thanking Frank for all the things he had done for the O's, I asked him if there was any place, any team, to which he would like to relocate. I assumed rightly that he would like to play for another couple of years, and as if he had previously thought through the matter, he quickly answered, "The Los Angeles Dodgers." I realized that in asking Frank where he would prefer to play, I severely limited my options, but I felt the Orioles owed him that courtesy, considering his great contribution to the franchise. I made my first sales call to LA, and in short order I was able to satisfy Robinson's request and traded him to the Dodgers. Right field was now vacant and Baylor was ready to fill the slot.

Winding down, Robby spent only one season with the Dodgers and was then traded across town to the Anaheim Angels, where he played for a couple of years before moving to the Cleveland Indians for a three-year stint. With his numbers decreasing annually, Robby agreed to be a player-manager for the Indians in 1975 and thus became the first African American manager in the Major

Leagues. Later voted into baseball's Hall of Fame in Cooperstown, Robinson had several other managerial jobs—with the Angels, Giants, Orioles, Expos, and Nationals. He also served as a special assistant to baseball commissioner Bud Selig.

After a hiatus year, the Orioles were back in the thick of the playoffs in 1973, winning the American League East, and then were matched against a good Oakland team, the best in the West. The five-game series was won by the Athletics, three games to two. Fire-balling Palmer won the first game, beating Vida Blue and shutting out the A's on just five hits in a 6–0 victory. Another memorable name on the A's pitching staff, Catfish Hunter, got his club even in the second game, winning 6–3, and the series moved to Oakland. Ken Holtzman, a stylish left-hander, went eleven innings for the home team in the next game for a 2–1 victory. Baltimore evened the series at two each the following day, 5–4, behind a bevy of relief pitchers. It all came to an end in the fifth game. Catfish Hunter pitched the A's to a 3–0 victory and sent the Birds packing back to Baltimore.

The very next year, the same two teams went at it again for the right to represent the American League in the World Series. The result was the same. Baltimore won the first game, but the A's came back to win the next three of the five, and the AL title. Mike Cuellar beat Catfish Hunter in the Oakland opener and they reversed roles in the fourth and final game, 2–1, in Baltimore.

Those '73 and '74 league championships were incredibly well played. The A's went on to win back-to-back World Series titles, topping the New York Mets, four games to three, in 1973, and the LA Dodgers, four games to one, the next year.

10

Negotiating Contracts

Like a presidential candidate picking a running mate, probably the biggest responsibility a GM has is to choose a field manager. I knew we had done a good job choosing Earl Weaver. Next, and carrying almost as much weight, is the task of player contract negotiation. Prior to the 1967 season and before the days when players had agents, the Orioles' staff did the negotiating. It was an interesting exercise, going one-on-one with the players. As one would imagine, some were tougher than others. Some were more unreasonable than others.

Dealing with Jim Palmer over the salary table always had an interesting dynamic. I never really tried to bargain with him. The session went something like this. "Jim, you had a great year. I think you are becoming the best pitcher in baseball. The scouts tell me the Mets have a great one in New York in Tom Seaver, but he is in the other league and I have never seen him over the course of a season. We know what you made last year. What do you think you are worth this year?" Palmer would inevitably come up with a figure that was higher than the one I had written down in my prospective budget. I would so inform him, but I would add that I would give him the benefit of the doubt this year and pay him what he had requested. "Remember this when we negotiate next year" would be my final salvo as we shook hands on the deal.

He would remember. The following season we would start out with the usual pleasantries, and then he would smile and confirm that he had received what he had requested the previous

{ 49

season and now it was my turn. As I recall, I never low-balled him, and in short order we had made another deal. I realize that all this seems almost too simple and even hard to believe, but that's exactly how it was with the Orioles and Jim Palmer. It was not always that easy. Some other players were more obstinate, some downright unrealistic.

Today's astronomical player salaries are totally out of hand. Even allowing for inflation, it's hard to justify a $3 or $4 million a year salary for a backup player, as is the case today. In 1973 O's future Hall of Fame third baseman Brooks Robinson earned a salary of $113,000. In 2013 Mets third baseman David Wright had a contract for $11 million for one year. Some rationalize that rock stars earn much more. That's true, but most brain surgeons don't come close to making that much, and I think the sense of proportion and value is way out of line.

50 } Ballplayers' agents have struck gold for their clients. But in many cases they have garnered a disproportionate amount of riches for themselves and sometimes given bad investment advice. I remember one agent, who represented Brooks Robinson and later Cal Ripken Jr. among others, who did give good advice. His basic message: Pay your taxes first, figure out how much you need to live on each year, and put the rest in tax-free municipal bonds.

Soaring salaries, of course, have inevitably led to higher ticket prices for fans, up more than ten times from a few decades ago, and, yes, enormous wealth for some team owners. A middle-class family of four cannot afford a lot of trips to the ballpark when they have to fork out three or four hundred dollars for tickets, refreshments, parking, and transportation for just one game. I worry that young people may not be able to afford these bewildering prices. For the future growth of baseball, we need to keep their interest alive and active.

Back with the Orioles, as salaries climbed, it became increasingly evident that the age of player agents was getting closer. For that reason, plus the fact that I felt we needed more help on the business side of the organization, I hired a young man, Al Harazin, who had been attached to the Minor League operation of the O's as owner of the team in Asheville, North Carolina.

A Chicago native, Harazin had gone to Drake University before transferring to Northwestern and eventually to the University of Michigan law school. He was practicing law for the prestigious Taft Stettinius & Hollister law firm in Cincinnati, and his wife, Ann, was a high school teacher. While still at the law firm, he attempted to satisfy a longtime urge to get into baseball. After a series of negative replies from Major League clubs, he purchased the aforementioned Orioles-affiliated Asheville team. Having secured that spot, he resigned from the law firm.

I tried to visit our top Minor League clubs every year, and the rest of them every other year. Having watched Al and Ann handle their American Association team for going on two years, I was convinced that Al would be a great help in Baltimore. He accepted { 51 the job I offered, sold his Minor League holding, and moved to the home office. It turned out to be one of the better deals I ever made. Al was the best baseball executive I ever worked with, and he excelled in virtually every facet of the game. Harazin's experience as a labor lawyer in Cincinnati was of immediate help in contract negotiations. One case stands out. A fairly young agent, Jerry Kapstein, one of the best in the business, notified us that he represented Bobby Grich and Don Baylor, by then two of our brightest young players. The new MLB labor contract, recently signed, provided for salary arbitration. If the club and the player could not agree on a contract, they could elect salary arbitration, in which both sides posted a salary number. After hearing both sides of the case, the arbitrator picked one or the other figure.

Grich was an excellent young player who had high salary expectations. The previous season he had sat out the first weeks of spring training over a $500 difference. In fact, this was a signal of his fierce competitiveness, the same competitiveness that made him the great ball player he became. When he was unable to reach an agreement with the O's on Grich's new contract, Kapstein became the first agent to file for salary arbitration. All of baseball—players, players' agents, executives, and owners—were paying close attention to the outcome. Grich had fine figures to argue. He was a Gold Glove infielder, had broken the all-time defensive record for MLB second basemen, but was a light hitter. Rather than seek outside professional help to assist our defense, Harazin and I, both lawyers, decided to argue the case ourselves as all baseball watched. I sat first chair and Harazin assisted.

One didn't have to be a genius to know that Kapstein's case would be based strongly on the phrase "record-setting second baseman." Therefore, in my opening statement I myself stipulated that Grich was an excellent defensive second baseman and had set an all-time mark at that position. But, I argued, it is regular offensive prowess that is the mark of the great, not defense. I even dragged up Ruth and Gehrig to illustrate my point. Every time Kapstein used the term "record-setting" or mentioned that accomplishment, I would spring up and remind the arbitrator that our side had already agreed to that and he was wasting everybody's time by bringing it up again. The arbitrator told me to sit down and not bring up any further objection. "You are being repetitive yourself. I noted your objection the first time you made it," he said. The arguments went back and forth for another hour until the man at the head table told us to "wrap things up."

52 }

I went second, behind Jerry, and my summation went something like this: "My worthy opponent has been regaling us with Mr. Grich's record-setting defensive performance and how it will forever impact all of big league baseball. If that is so, Mr. Kapstein, so knowledgeable about Major League baseball, will you please instruct our judge as to who is the current record-setting defensive first baseman and the shortstop, and who holds that honor at third base?" Watching his jaw drop and his whole head follow, I heard him grudgingly admit that he didn't know. After offering the answer to my own question, I suggested that those defensive marks couldn't be that important if nobody remembered them. I rested our case. In fairly short order, the arbitrator ruled in our favor.

My ability to handle myself in arbitration matters would not have happened had it not been for a nocturnal exercise of attending law school for four and a half years in the late 1950s.

It's one thing to get out of law school; it's another and more important thing to pass your state bar exam. You can't practice law until you do so. The Maryland state tests came up in March, which left scant time for cramming. I decided to ignore the odds and give it a try. I don't remember the exact dates, but results came out about six weeks after the test.

Only a few law school graduates pass the bar exam on the first try. For some it takes two; for others, three, four, or even five tries. This is nervous time. The results came in the mail, and most would-be lawyers take the day off to greet the mailman and be the first to learn their fate. That didn't appeal to me, so I set out for work as usual, telling my wife to call me when the official letter arrived. But it was early in the morning and Jean didn't seem too happy about her assignment. I called home in the late morning and asked, "Have you opened it?" Her negative response was followed by a firm declaration that I should come home and open it myself. I assured her that the result was not going to change whether she opened it or I came all the way home and opened the letter myself. She reluctantly agreed and there was a long silence, punctuated by the sound of a letter being opened. Then in a humorless and deeply sarcastic voice she blurted out, "You passed—but it's the only damn bar you've passed since we got married." (Despite this, and similar treatment from time to time, we're still together today, some sixty-plus years later.)

Back in the baseball arbitration arena, Jerry Kapstein and I had several more salary tussles, but the Grich experience always remained in mind, if not in our conversations. Strange as it seems, Jerry and I became friends of a sort. I think it was mutual ad-

{ 53

miration more than anything else. Jerry had graduated from Harvard and had an encyclopedic knowledge of baseball. I had unsuccessfully challenged him several times to get out of the agency business and into running a professional baseball team.

At the same time, my wife, Jean, urged me to get into the agency game, thinking it a more lucrative pursuit than running a ball club. As usual, she was absolutely right, and I often wondered how my life would have played out if I had made the change, although I never really considered it.

There was one incident in Baltimore when, for some agonizing minutes, I feared there might not be any future with the Orioles. I took no bows but did take the blows. It had a lasting effect on me. I never publicly reported it, over concern that the incident would be repeated. But it is indelibly etched in memory.

The Orioles were playing the Minnesota Twins in a postseason playoff for the American League title in 1970. This was a new phenomenon at that time—a playoff game where the Eastern and Western division winners played each other for the right to represent their league in the World Series. It happened in Baltimore at old Memorial Stadium, early in the game, a tight one, I remember. But then most of these playoff contests were close encounters. I was sitting in my private box in the press area when I got a telephone call from the Oriole office down below. "Mr. Cashen," came the voice of this veteran telephone lady, "the police are here and they want to talk to you. They said they need you here as quickly as possible," and she hung up. Nothing further. But I could tell by the tone of her voice that it was urgent.

When I got to my office, I found that a number of people were already gathered at the secretary's desk. Although some were outfitted in civilian garb and some in full uniform, it quickly turned out that all were members of the Baltimore City Police Department. A uniformed captain appeared to be the leader of the onslaught and lost little time in getting to the point. "Mr. Cashen," he explained, "the Baltimore City Police Department has been notified by phone that a major bomb has been placed in this stadium and is reported to be set to go off during the baseball game." I was bewildered; there is no other word to describe my reaction.

He continued, "You must make a decision whether to stop the game and clear the stadium."

"And what do you suggest?" I blurted out, looking around at a forest of grim faces.

"We don't suggest; the matter is entirely up to you," he retorted, "and it must be done promptly."

I was aware that bomb threats were not uncommon in those days. In fact, it got to be almost a game some younger people were playing. It would be a major victory for the conspirators if we stopped the game and cleared the stadium; that much was clear to me immediately. But what happens if I don't heed the warning and the stadium blows up and thousands die? It was confusing to say the least, but I counseled myself to slow down, concentrate, and give the men in blue an answer.

I understood the police's unwillingness to make a decision. Early on in these matters, they had been closing down the bulk of the businesses so threatened and came in for acute criticism when nothing happened. That's when they figured out that it should be up to those who had the most at stake to make the decision. It all seemed a bit unfair to me but I knew that I had to say something, and with more conviction than I really felt, I spoke up. "Let's ignore the phone call, let the game go on, leave the stands intact, and pray for the best." The police crowd broke up, but some didn't go far away and I had the distinct feeling they were keeping me in sight. The captain stayed around for a while making small talk, and I realized later that he was just trying to calm me down. What followed was probably the worst two and a half hours of my life.

Once alone, a torrent of questions swept over me. Should I have asked for someone's advice before the hasty decision? But whose? Did I owe it to Jerry Hoffberger to seek his opinion before

I ignored the threat? How about the commissioner of baseball? Didn't he have a lot to do with deciding whether or not the game should continue? What would it mean to other clubs? It would have been nice to have the time to talk to the others involved, but the police said there was no time for that. They needed an immediate answer.

Suddenly I had no interest in the outcome of the playoff game. I remember searching my mind for the most likely place a bomb could be planted. Surely not out in the field. If there was one, it had to be here near the offices, which were in the catacombs under the stands. I wanted to get as close as possible to where the blast would be, hoping it would kill me first. I could never live with the knowledge that I could have stopped the game and cleared the stadium.

But was sealing my own fate fair to my family? Was I first selfishly, and perhaps even foolishly, choosing to die? My legal training clicked in about then and I began to think about the lawsuits that were certain to follow. Wouldn't the National Brewing Company, which was the principal owner of the team, bear the brunt of the legal claims? I was employed by the ball club, which was owned by the brewery. If people were killed or maimed, certainly the police would point out that I had made the decision. The result of all this agony made me start second-guessing my decision, and for me there was nothing left to do but pray. And I sure did!

All of the torment went for naught, of course. The O's and Twins finished the game and the sellout crowd filed out of the stadium without incident. I don't even remember who won. I agreed with the police that if we acknowledged the incident, we would have similar crank bomb calls for the next five years. Few people ever heard of the incident. But that's the way it was. Thankfully, I never had to deal with that kind of threat at Shea Stadium when I was with the Mets.

My ten years running the Orioles proved to be the most successful such period in the club's history. While I was chief operating officer, we were in four World Series—1966, 1969, 1970, and 1971—and two American League championship series—losing to Charley Finley's Oakland club in '73 and '74. The 1969 World Series loss to the New York Mets was the most difficult to stomach. The following year, of course, we beat Cincinnati for the world title and then, in 1971, we lost to the Pittsburgh Pirates in a hard-fought seven games, as described.

Most satisfying to me and to Baltimore fans, the Orioles had become habitual postseason contestants. Over the decade, the O's finished first or second every season but two. Playing winning baseball every season but 1967, the Orioles won more than ninety games in seven of those seasons and more than a hundred games in three. Attendance soared and we averaged just above or just below a million each season. Baseball was back in Baltimore. We had put the club on solid footing and strengthened our Minor League teams. One of my good picks was drafting Eddie Murray { 57 in the third round of the 1973 amateur draft. After several years in the Minors, the switch-hitting first baseman joined the O's and began a twenty-one-year Major League career and later was elected to baseball's Hall of Fame.

Baltimore Orioles great Cal Ripken Jr., the Iron Man, came along after my time with the O's, along with his brother, Billy, also a MLB ballplayer. His father, Cal Sr., worked for me when I joined the O's in 1966. Cal Sr. was a very good Minor League manager and ran a special camp for Minor Leaguers. When he asked for the chance to come to the parent club, we were able to offer him the job of first base coach. He joined the O's coaching staff and served with distinction for many years, including a brief time as manager in the late 1980s. Altogether, Cal Sr. served in the Orioles organization—Majors and Minors—for thirty-six years. Having grown up in a baseball family, Cal Jr. had lived with his parents in many places and knew the game backward and forward. One of three sons, Cal Jr. was drafted by my successor in Baltimore, Hank Peters, a year after I left for the Mets and debuted with the

Orioles in 1981. During his twenty-one seasons with the O's, Cal broke Lou Gehrig's "iron man" record for consecutive games played and became one of only eight players at the time to hit more than 400 home runs and top 3,000 hits. His astounding run brought joy to Baltimore fans and greatly enriched baseball history.

My First Passion

As I closed out my very happy years with the Orioles, I realized that it was a long way from my first career passion—newspapering. I would go from a high school newspaper to a job as a copy boy at the *Baltimore News-Post*, to an apprentice city desk man, then the sports department as an all-around "gopher," and finally a chance to write—as a reporter and a sportswriter. At that time I felt, "Who could ask for anything more?" I was in heaven. Ready for more? Well, here's the continuing story. {59

It was still wartime, 1945, and college had taken twenty-five months and one day, start to finish. Freshman, sophomore, junior, and senior years were accelerated, so that year we were the fastest group ever to get through Loyola College (now University) in Baltimore. I had a double major—philosophy and English. My extracurricular activities included one as sports editor of the school paper, the *Greyhound*; college debate team member; B-team basketball player; and the sixteenth man on the baseball squad as I've mentioned before, a weak-armed, light-hitting, and questionable defensive second baseman.

Coming up short athletically convinced me that I would be more successful writing about sports than playing them. Confirmation came soon enough. Graduation was on a Sunday. The next day at 6:45 a.m., I reported to the local Hearst newspaper, the *Baltimore News-Post*, where, as previously described, I had worked as a copy boy. This time, I would be a full-time sportswriter.

It was July of that last year of World War II. In two months I would be twenty. Earlier, after I turned eighteen, I had signed up for the Naval Air Corps, but I ultimately failed the eye exam. When the Korean War broke out in 1950, I was ultimately drafted and passed the physical for the army, but I did not have to go on active duty because I was by then married with two children. So I batted .000 for my military career.

But back to my new job as a sportswriter. In 1945 things were not the way they are now. There were no computers, and you showed up by 7 a.m. to write—on a manual typewriter—whatever assignment you had covered the night before. The first edition of the afternoon paper came out at 11 a.m., followed by three more. The final edition, especially noted for the late horse race results, came out at 5 p.m.

It wasn't always fun. One quickly learned to sit in on the sports copy desk, make up a late edition and complete a dozen other small assignments. With a lifelong interest in horse racing, I was soon assigned the chore of picking the daily horse results in the feature tracks of the season. "Tred Avon" was given to me as my picking label card, and like the other handicappers, I kept track of the local ponies with a collection of racing charts assembled from the various racing papers—the *Daily Racing Form* and the *Morning Telegraph*. As you can quickly surmise, there is no certainty in picking horses. You develop your own little tricks—and "tricks" is the appropriate word. While I never was much of a bettor, I developed a personal affection for horse racing beyond my journalistic interest.

I was a great believer in breeding and always favored the lower half of the breed over the upper half—translated, I usually favored the mares' breeding over the getup of the stud. This approach made for a longer time in the selection process, but I always felt it was worth it.

Life at the newspaper then was worlds away from today's computerized media scene. Even television was still in its infancy.

Art Janney, the *News-Post*'s assistant sports editor, really ran the department. Roger Pippen, an old codger who had the title of sports editor, showed up every morning at the same time, not until 7:45 a.m., wrote a disjointed daily column, hung around till after the first edition surfaced, and then was gone for the day, usually to a local golf course. A veteran of the trade, Pippen had known a lot of old-time sports stars like Ty Cobb and Babe Ruth and was never bashful telling you about them. Art Janney, though, was the guts of our business and kept a close but kindly hand on this young writer. We had a big Sunday morning paper, the *American*, and between the daily and the Sunday editions, Saturday was an action-packed venture.

I had helped John Steadman, a buddy of mine from our caddying days, to get a job at the paper. He had played a year of professional baseball in the Pittsburgh Pirates' system and got to love the newspaper business as much as I did. On Monday mornings, after the hectic weekend schedule, Janney would take Steadman and me aside, along with any other young talent he had assembled, to go over the past week's work. Janney was like a college professor, gently but firmly pointing out flaws and explaining how one was overusing certain words, praising other habits but constantly reminding us that our material had to be consistently honest. He would say, "Just as it would be in the Bible, you have to build up a confidence with your readers. If you write it, they believe it."

Whether it was because of Janney's efforts or because practice should make perfect, a succession of awards in the Hearst papers competition would indicate that my scribbling was improving substantially. The National Basketball Writers decided that one of my columns—which was about Frank McGuire, then basketball coach at the University of North Carolina—was the best of the year and merited first prize. That prize turned out to be a pair of first-class field binoculars. I never figured out the relevance of such an award given for a column on basketball, but I accepted

{ 61

willingly and put them to good use in covering football, lacrosse, and horse racing.

In 1955 my piece about the Navy football team, "The Football Team Named Desire," and its appearance in the Sugar Bowl in New Orleans, took one of the top prizes in the annual Best Sports Stories of the Year. Although several other writing prizes followed, none brought me more satisfaction than that piece on the Middie footballers.

But back again to my day-to-day career. At the *News-Post* in the late fifties, I was active in the in-house union, the Editorial News Union of Baltimore. That activity, such as it was, led to my election as president of the union, and hence head of the negotiating committee. My feeling had always been, "I love this business and I really don't care what they pay me." But, it became abundantly clear that the wages, even at the top of the salary scale, were going to be insufficient for my growing family. All this led me to tackle the University of Maryland School of Law. I fought a four-year night school tussle and won a JD, a doctorate in law. There was, however, a revealing interruption along the way.

During the first semester of my third year, Ed Hayes, the sports editor of the Hearst-owned *Detroit Times*, called and offered me a job as a daily columnist for his paper. We had pretty well worked out the particulars and Hayes indicated he needed a final answer in two weeks. They were a busy two weeks. After talking it over with my wife, Jean, I was ready to accept the job. She began prepping our house for sale and our kids for the move. The *News-Post* was surprised by my impending departure, but my colleagues were quick to express their good wishes.

The same day I gave the *News-Post* my letter of resignation and the reason I was fleeing to Detroit, I went to the University of Maryland School of Law and transferred my credits to a similar school at the University of Detroit. Having started the whole exercise because of my interest in labor law, part of my resolve in making the switch centered on Detroit as a much more promising field for what I considered to be my future specialty. Hayes seemed delighted with the news that I was headed for the Motor City.

We began to inform friends and family of our imminent departure, counseled with the real estate agent, and did the countless other little things that become necessary when one makes a major move. The deflating news came less than a week later. My wife phoned to tell me that Ed Hayes had been calling our house. He had left messages, including a list of phone numbers, saying he needed to talk to me as soon as possible.

When I returned the call, Ed first asked if I had heard anything from the publisher of the *News-Post*. I remember joking and telling him that my departure was not significant enough even to be noted by Fred Archibald, our publisher. "That's where you're wrong," Hayes shot back, and proceeded to tell me the rest of the tale. The *Detroit Times* was forced to withdraw its offer of employment, Hayes informed me, after being advised by "Hearst higher-ups in New York." That's what he told me, although it was, he said, the Detroit paper that actually pulled the plug.

What happened was that when the fact of my departure reached Archibald, he protested to headquarters that allowing one Hearst paper to hire a writer from another Hearst paper for a sizable pay increase was no way to run a chain of newspapers. Apparently, the "higher-ups" agreed, and to avoid any further conflict, the Detroit paper canceled the offer. Hayes and I eventually talked at length but we couldn't understand what had happened. I had thought that the Baltimore management would be glad to be rid of me because of my union activities. The publisher, although not a party at the negotiating table, was actually the power behind the management side, and evidently concluded that my services to the paper overrode my representation of the working stiffs.

So, I went back to work at the *News-Post* and, yes, at no increase in salary. But I had renewed interest in getting my law degree and moving on to bigger and better things.

One additional newspaper job opportunity came up before

I put the final cover on my typewriter. In my opinion, the *New York Herald-Tribune* had the best sportswriting staff in the country. When their veteran basketball writer was assigned to cover yachting and had to forgo his roundball duties, I was encouraged by a staffer to indicate my interest in the job. "We know they are interested in you," he promised. Moving my family to New York, or at least the environs, was not high on my "happy-to-do list" and I dismissed the matter from my mind.

Both the Detroit and New York papers were eventually victims of the newspaper carnage, which left me pleased with my decision to finish law school. Having lost a half-year while planning to relocate, it took me four and a half years to complete final classes, which I did in late January of 1958. Saturday classes allowed me to keep my concentration on labor law throughout, although a course in admiralty law, taught by Dean Roger Howell in my final year, also caught my interest. I promised myself that if anything precluded my taking a shot at labor law, I'd be sure to look into admiralty.

The time between finishing classes in January of 1958 and picking up the diploma in June was not wasted. Prepping for the March bar exam while still working in the newspaper business was certainly intense, but once that was behind me I began interviewing. In fact, I had already talked to several people in the labor law business. Their advice had been consistent and it all boiled down to this: Try to get a slot with the National Labor Relations Board (NLRB) and spend a couple years learning the bible of labor. Then you'll have a handful of options in no particular order. You could join a firm of labor lawyers or stay with the NLRB. You could set up your own labor firm; join a general law firm as a labor specialist; or go to work for a major business firm in its labor relations department. But all the above advice emphasized the need first to have a solid background with the NLRB.

Taking the advice of the majority, I submitted a written application and then contacted the NLRB in Washington, recited my qualifications, and succeeded in getting a job interview. I was directed to an official who seemed as anxious as I was for the interview. He waved my written application in one hand while directing me to a seat facing his rather large and imposing desk. His very first question was about my sportswriting history. He asked if I had had any experience with the Baltimore Colts.

It turned out that he was a major Colts fan, with season tickets, who seemed to live and die with the team. When I told him I worked in the press box during the Colts' home games and had a one-on-one relationship with a bunch of the veteran players, he confessed to being a longtime fan and said he lived in nearby Annapolis. Alan Ameche, the All-American fullback from the University of Wisconsin, was his favorite Colts player. He then quit the football conversation as quickly as he had started it and once again took up my application.

It was evident from the start that he had read my written history carefully and was somewhat impressed, though he didn't seem to understand why I would want to leave sportswriting for a spot as a labor lawyer. To be honest, I was beginning to question it myself. We had an intense conversation about my experience as president of the labor union at the newspaper, my negotiation experience, and my ability to both write and speak on the subject. Just when I felt he was going to give me a stamp of approval, he went back to football chatter. { 65

I spent almost an hour with the gentleman and I am sure both of us enjoyed the encounter. In the final moments of our set-to, he offered me a job, but cautioned that it started at the low government pay scale and that I would be responsible for getting myself and my family to our first assignment. He added that if I was subsequently moved to another site, as was the custom, the government would handle the expenses.

Jean and I consulted on the latest job offer, and the lure of labor law lessened with the knowledge that we would probably have to sell our house in Baltimore, move husband, wife, and three children to a then unknown destination—and all for less money than I was already making. It didn't take long to decide that the NLRB job was a loser in this contest.

Having been so courteously and graciously interviewed, I decided that the official deserved more than a phone call or letter notifying him of my change of heart. I phoned his office and set up another appointment. And knowing that my NLRB dream was ended, my subsequent journey back to Washington was somewhat sad. It was then I remembered an old question. "Are you troubled with regrets?" it asked, and I could only answer in the affirmative. Why hadn't I researched the U.S. government's starting salaries? What were the practices regarding moving a new employee to the job site? I second-guessed myself. And the next question I asked myself was "Why had I wasted four and a half years on law school for this?" I was indeed troubled with regrets.

66 } My interviewer friend was immensely helpful once again. He was sorry for my decision to forgo the offer but seemed sympathetic to my reasoning. He followed up with an inquiry about whether things would have been different if I worked in Washington and spent a couple of years commuting from Baltimore. "Why do you ask?" I inquired. He knew someone who was starting a new government agency in Washington and was currently looking for staff lawyers. It would be called the National Aeronautics and Space Administration. There would be a need, he continued, for people who could write and who could go up to Capitol Hill to suck money from Congress as things got going. If you have any interest, he added, I'll be happy to give my friend a call and set up an interview. I'm sure he will give you every consideration for the new agency.

Let's recall that the Russians had sent up Sputnik the year before, but that was all I knew of space. In fact, it was pretty much all that many knew about a space program. But I thanked him profusely, promised to keep in touch, and headed back to Baltimore. Jean and I discussed the matter, which we called the

"Buck Rogers opportunity," and quickly decided we were not interested. Thanks, but no thanks, and we promptly turned to opportunities in our hometown.

Notwithstanding this initial disappointment, I found later that a law degree was an enormous advantage. As for newspapering, I treasured my days with the *Baltimore News-Post* and appreciate the important role of the printed word, even in this increasingly digital world.

12

From Studs to Suds

Before I got into baseball in 1966, I had two other, very different, career pursuits. Both were thanks to Baltimore business leader Jerry Hoffberger. Having already threatened to step away from the newspaper business and having dropped the idea of a career in labor, I met with an old friend, Joe Lynch, a former FBI guy. He was then running the local harness track, the Baltimore Raceway.

Over a couple of scotches, we talked. Principally, he wanted to tell me that Jerry Hoffberger was interested in discussing job opportunities with me. Jerry was president and chairman of the board of the popular National Brewing Company.

I didn't understand what this was all about, but I readily agreed to talk to the raceway boss. Joe set up the appointment and I went off to visit Hoffberger, whom I had not previously met. I did know of his first-rate reputation, however. As I remember, the thrust of the encounter was simply to get acquainted, and most of the time was spent talking about Hoffberger's thoroughbred horse holdings. So I was somewhat surprised when, on the spot, he offered me a job as assistant general manager of the harness track, with Lynch as my boss.

I had the feeling that Joe was the moving instrument in this whole scenario, had plotted it all out, and knew in advance that he was to have a new assistant. As for me, it was a lifetime hookup with Hoffberger, who offered me quite a few jobs during our lengthy friendship.

I then left the *News-Post*, which was to survive only a few more years before merging with the *Baltimore American*. That merged paper lasted another twenty years and finally folded in 1986.

Either Joe Lynch was an excellent teacher of the racetrack business or I was a fast learner, but whatever the combination, we hit it off right away. Dave Herman, whose public relations firm worked with quite a few racetracks, including Baltimore Raceway, was a fixture, but I soon picked up the media duties and got positive responses from the newspaper crowd. As a result we managed to get a good sendoff when we headed south to the winter training sites.

This venture took us to training tracks in the Carolinas and Georgia before reaching our ultimate target—Ben White Raceway, outside Orlando, Florida. The purpose of our trip was to persuade the trainers to include our track in their thirty-day summer circuit. To further entice them we had set up a series of stake races for their younger horses. We nicknamed them the Lord and Lady Baltimore Stakes, the former, of course, for colts and the latter for the fillies.

Some of the good but less famous stables were in the Carolinas—Pinehurst and Southern Pines, with a couple of entries in nearby Tennessee. Joe passed on all this knowledge to me as we traveled but insisted that the best stables were in Florida. Del Miller, the pride of Washington, Pennsylvania, was the number one guy in the business. He bred, and along with the Hanover Shoe Farm, he annually produced the best of the breed. Billy Haughton, who at this time was as good a driver as Miller, did his racing in New York, and a young horseman named Stanley Dancer had an excellent stable and competed out of New Egypt, New Jersey.

With Lynch leading the parade, buying the drinks, and holding first-class dinner feasts, these titans of the harness world responded to our message. They provided some excellent young stock for our stake races, and part of their string of stables, albeit

{ 69

a lesser part except for the young stake horses also camped on our grounds.

It was evident to me as the season ran its course that Joe was meant for bigger and better things. When he announced at the end of my first season that he was leaving Baltimore Raceway, I was not surprised. And before I had time to think about it, I was notified that I would take over as general manager. Harness racing had never really succeeded in Baltimore, which only caused me to strengthen my resolve to take the job. As if that was not a big enough challenge, there was more to come. The group of owners of Baltimore Raceway, which featured harness racing, purchased the local Bel Air Race Track, a thoroughbred operation located about twenty miles north of Baltimore City. Maryland had a number of county tracks that included Timonium, Cumberland, and Hagerstown. One of these tracks was Bel Air, a three-quarter-mile oval that also staged the Harford County Fair during its short, twelve-day racing season.

At the harness track the previous season, I had become acquainted with Tom Hoffecker, a former All-American lacrosse goalie at the University of Maryland, who had a farm in the horse country of Baltimore County. He became a valuable assistant with the trotters and doubled that value with the thoroughbred crowd. Tom had a string of ponies for his three daughters and was well known to the horsey set. He and I had comparatively little trouble with the race meet.

The majority of the local thoroughbred stables were in that circuit of half-mile tracks, and the racing secretary was great at filling the daily race card. Some of the other pros seemed to have periodic breakdowns and it sometimes fell to me to make the morning line or assist the morning clocker. In retrospect, it was a pleasurable stint. The morning line established the early betting odds on the races. It was subject to change once the mutuel betting windows opened and was in constant flux until the individual race was run. There was a flood of horses working out at the track every morning. And those who were obviously getting ready to officially compete in the near future were timed (hence the name morning clocker) over a distance of ground (for example, five furlongs), and that was noted as part of the published form.

Running the Harford County Fair, however, was something else. For a city-raised guy it was a great unknown. The milk cattle people were different from the beef cattle people, and meeting both groups for the first time was a problem. Tom and I had prepared by literally spending hours quizzing each other on the names in the program and whatever information we had gathered on the farmers. And we lived through it and, if I may say so, in excellent style. (One of the better parts was running the annual Miss Harford County contest that brought together a host of comely county girls vying for the crown. We had veteran county personalities as judges, which we hoped would get us out of the firing line.) { 71 All in all, it was an interesting experience—the thoroughbred races, the Miss Harford County contest, the cattle judging, the competition to see who made the best jelly in the county, and a host of other events. But we were happy when it was over.

Horses and horse racing had never been far from my mind, and my time at the Bel Air Track rekindled the spark. At this time I was firmly convinced that when I retired from ordinary pursuits, I would go back to the thoroughbred tracks and see if I could make a go of it with a small string of racehorses.

Later on, to keep my hand in that industry while being employed elsewhere, I purchased a couple of potential broodmares. Both were by a horse named Occupy, a stud horse I considered to be worthwhile. They were stabled on Tommy Hoffecker's farm. The puzzle of where and to which studs to breed our young mares was a constant problem and involved a great degree of study and, ultimately, what is best described as guessing. Bloodlines were the subject of the exercise and availability the final piece of the puzzle. The first year both mares came up barren, and the next season one of the two produced a foal and the other disappointed again, making her zero for two.

Meanwhile, Jean was much more successful. She kept getting pregnant while the mares proved to be what in horse parlance are known as "shy breeders." I was convinced I had things wrong, so I sold the mares, got out of the horse business, and redoubled my dedication to family.

In telling the four-legged part of my sports story, I'm reminded that early on I had been warned that both of our racetracks were in play, but the announcement that our racing interests had been sold was, nevertheless, a stunner. Convinced that a thirty-day harness meet and a twelve-day thoroughbred allowance were not sufficient to make a profit, the owners had gone to our statewide brethren in like endeavors and stated bluntly, "We will buy you out, or you buy us out." In the end the latter prevailed. In essence, what we sold were the dates, while we retained the premises. Thus, actual racing became someone else's problem, and I have often joked that I was so successful in running the tracks that today they are both strip shopping malls.

Before the sale of the racing dates was announced, Jerry Hoffberger had offered me a job as his administrative assistant at the brewery. It was a seamless transition. It took me a short time to clean up in the two track offices and I reported promptly to the National Brewing Company. Several out-of-state offers to go back into the harness track business followed, but I gave them scant consideration and directed all my efforts to learning the beer business.

The first couple of assignments were interesting. I looked at a successful racetrack in New Jersey and a small brewery in Pennsylvania. Both, so we heard, were for sale. Both were worth a gamble, I reported, and later were sold, but not to the National Brewing Company. I don't think we made a bid on either. Independent breweries in Miami, St. Louis, Detroit, and Tacoma, Washington, had fallen prey to Hoffberger's growing expansion thirst, but through no effort on my part. I was still settling into my new position when Hoffberger summoned me to his office and challenged me with yet another new assignment. This one was new all right—and utterly surprising.

The director of advertising had just been fired for some reason or other and Hoffberger exclaimed, "You are going upstairs to run the advertising department!"

He could have hit me over the head with a beer barrel. I was dumbfounded. "But I don't know anything about advertising," I protested. I did know that the brewery had always had first-class advertising in the newspapers and on the radio and particularly on TV, which was a relatively new medium at the time. The newly fired advertising manager, whom I later learned was axed for imbibing too often in a different colored and more potent beverage than beer, had done a good job. He had gotten the brewery's "From the Land of Pleasant Living" ad campaign off and running in high style.

All this flooded my mind as I stood, dazed and unbelieving, in the boss's office. I do remember him saying I would be fine and that a big corner office awaited me upstairs. He added that if I had a real problem, I should give him a buzz and he would be glad to help. Staggering out of Jerry's office, I was congratulated and embraced by his attractive secretary, who apparently knew what was to come before I did. The enormity of what had just happened continued to amaze me, as did Hoffberger's confidence in me to handle yet another of so many different assignments.

There was no break-in period on this one, and I was in the ad office the next day. My limited knowledge of the beer business whispered to me that, other than the president and coo of the brewery, the brewmaster and the director of advertising were the next two most important jobs. The brewmaster, of course, oversaw how the product was made while the ad director's principal function was to get the product sold. My annual ad budget that first year was roughly $14 million, which was more money than Major League Baseball teams were selling for at that time. A one-year budget of $14 million!

I have often wondered how Hoffberger could have given me such wonderful assignments—operating race tracks, working as his administrative assistant, director of advertising of his breweries, director of marketing of the Baltimore Orioles, and shortly thereafter chief executive of that Major League Baseball team. And then, ten years later, senior vice president of sales and marketing of the Carling Breweries. Jerry and I became friends, of course, close friends, but I never let that interfere with my work. He must have known things about me that I didn't know myself. I think I did understand Jerry and knew what made him tick. His love for his wife, Alice, and their three sons and a daughter, along with his philanthropic pursuits in local and international Jewish fields, was evident indeed. He also was well known in professional sports.

To my way of thinking, it wasn't the Orioles, or his earlier minority interest in the hugely successful Baltimore Colts football franchise, or the Baltimore Bays pro soccer team, that piqued Hoffberger's interest. It was the horse racing business. He had always kept a few horses at his home in Brooklandville, but when he sold the Orioles, he bought a 120-acre spread in nearby Howard County and got serious about the breeding business. How serious? From Ireland he purchased one of the most successful studs in the world, Run the Gauntlet, who already had produced money winners in some of the world's top distance stakes.

With a full slate of quality mares booked for that first season in the United States, things were looking excellent for the breeding business. But disaster struck in an almost unbelievable fashion. While servicing the very first mare he had been matched with in this country, the big fella, Run the Gauntlet, had a heart attack, slid to the ground, and died on the stable floor. Jerry's horse breeding venture never fully recovered.

Fortunately, for me coming into a new job, National Brewing was served by a strong and unique advertising agency. The W. B. Donor Agency, headquartered in Detroit but with a strong presence in Baltimore, was headed by Herb Fried, a young and clever practitioner of the ad business. Herb and I got along well (an advantage to us both) and soon became fast friends. We had a couple of products the brewery was developing. One in particular was Colt 45, a malt liquor that was stronger than beer and that we felt had infinite possibilities. Colt 45, in large part because of a good ad campaign, got off to a fast start and is still around today.

Aside from the eye-popping budgets, advertising was an exciting business. It got my creative juices flowing and challenged my decision making while molding my ability to run a major business with a sizable budget. I enjoyed my time with the brewmasters and absolutely loved the advertising game.

13

Commish's Call

Returning to the story of my baseball years, changes in my life were in the works in the mid-1970s. I had gotten to know Bowie Kuhn, a Princeton and University of Virginia law school graduate who since had represented the National League as its outside counsel. He was a member of the Wilke Farr firm in New York, assigned to their National League account. With the help of his close friend Walter O'Malley, owner of the Los Angeles Dodgers, Bowie was elected as the fifth commissioner of baseball in 1969, at a time when rivalry between the American and National leagues continued to be intense. Bowie, of course, resigned from the law firm when he became commissioner.

Bowie and his wife, Louisa, were raising three teenagers while living in New Jersey. And very often when the entire Kuhn family went on a baseball outing, they headed for Baltimore. We treated them royally in every way, including the chance to watch top-flight baseball. The Kuhns seemed to like our postgame antics too. After the game, the bar was always open in my office, and with a brewery as the team's principal owner, that bar never seemed to run dry.

When I left the baseball club in 1976 to return to National Brewing at Jerry Hoffberger's request, Bowie expressed his surprise and disappointment. But the Hoffberger family had planned to sell the brewery and Jerry thought somehow that I could help put a better face on the business. It was soon sold to Carling Red Cap of Canada and then shortly after that to South African interests. I then began to view my role as less satisfying. So in 1978 when

I was offered a job as administrator of baseball in the commissioner's office—which in effect was the number two position in all baseball—I accepted, and early in 1979 I packed my bags and headed for New York.

It became immediately apparent that Bowie Kuhn was not only willing but also anxious to pass some of his duties off to a lesser light. Anything that pertained to the playing of the game was to be handled by the administrator. Bowie dealt with the owners, the lawyers, and the law. My additional duties included running the weekly staff meetings, where problems within the game were discussed and, hopefully, solved. The staff seemed to respond well to me, their new leader. Soon after, we began to focus on the upcoming All-Star Game. Seattle, a comparatively new team, was scheduled to host, and after brief discussions, Bowie told me that the All-Star Game was the responsibility of the commissioner and that I was to set up a series of visits to { 77 Seattle to prepare for the event.

Neither Seattle's general manager, my old pal Lou Gorman, nor manager Darrell Johnson had ever been exposed to running an All-Star Game, and Bowie was somewhat cautious about what role Danny Kaye, the Hollywood star and one of the owners of the Mariners, would want to play. In fact, Kaye proved to be a real gem. All he wanted was to get on the big league bench an hour prior to the game, watch batting practice, and talk baseball. The All-Star Game came off without a hitch.

It was about this time when the commissioner's office was lobbied by Rachel Robinson. Commissioner Kuhn always held Robinson, the widow of Jackie Robinson, in the highest regard. Accordingly, he was responsive to her suggestions. Late in the 1970s, Rachel had cornered Bowie about why, despite the high number of African American players in the Majors, only a few were working in administration. It took only a brief look at the record to prove that Mrs. Robinson was correct.

Kuhn, ever the do-gooder, put together a small, unofficial group of baseball executives and quickly came up with a plan. Major League Baseball would establish scholarships at St. John's University in the New York borough of Queens for young African American males to attend the school's athletics administration program. Further, Bowie's office would make every effort to place the graduates with various big league teams. The cost of the program was to be split between the two New York clubs—the Mets and the Yankees. In 1979, as one of the lieutenants in Kuhn's army, I was particularly—and enthusiastically—involved.

Because it was limited to members of a special group, we couldn't make the program part of a public school offering. But we preached our gospel to the city and environs as best we could. I doubt that any African American student in those places was unaware of baseball's scholarship offer. We were surprised and disappointed

when that first graduating class did not produce a single applicant. So we decided to triple our efforts in the future. In the end, after getting what proved to be zero interest from African American high school males, the committee redesigned the program to include all minorities. It then became wonderfully successful, especially once it was known that women were considered minorities. An overwhelming sea of applications flowed in and the Hispanic populations followed suit. So the problem was solved, though not in the way that Rachel Robinson had suggested.

Years later, with the popularity of the program going well beyond the New York market, Peter Ueberroth, by that time commissioner, ruled that the program would be funded by all the clubs, not just the Mets and the Yankees. As the original system began to slow down, the Jackie Robinson Scholarship Program reached different and greater heights. There are now Jackie Robinson scholarships awarded each year, one for each of the Major League clubs. They are awarded to worthy minority recipients and allow them to follow their hearts into whatever career they seek—in medicine, law, banking, and, sometimes, even baseball.

Another talent search in which the commissioner's office was involved called for all the Major League clubs to select at least two of the best résumés they had received over the past year from college seniors looking for jobs in baseball. All of these were then presented to a veterans committee that whittled the pile down to eight. The lucky eight were then invited to New York to interview before another top committee. The two who finished on top in this final drill received a year's paid internship in baseball. Once hired, they spent time in the commissioner's office, the two league offices, Major League properties, the labor relations department, and, of course, a brief spot with a Major League team. Suffice it to say, they were exposed to all facets of the game.

This all started more than thirty years ago, and I still remember that the top candidate that first year was a young lady who wowed us all with her obvious talent. Subsequent years produced at least two young professionals who today are now veteran general managers of big league clubs. Mark that ambitious program as successful. { 79

Years ago, as now, I was always willing to talk baseball, both the good and the bad of the game. One thing that always had troubled me was that most of the people who worked in professional baseball, other than players and umpires, had no retirement system. The Major League players' union had built a sparkling retirement plan and the umpires had followed suit.

Early in my time in the commissioner's office, I advised Bowie about the subject and asked for permission to try to get something started. He quickly gave permission and I went to work. Remember at this point, some employees had worked all their adult lives in baseball and had left the game with no financial rewards. More than a few old-timers had spent twenty, thirty, or even forty years working in the game and retired with a handshake and an "attaboy," but no pension. One of those, I recall, was Jim McLauglin, who had toiled for the St. Louis Browns, Baltimore Orioles, and Cincinnati Reds and had mentored a crowd of young Oriole executives through the intricacies of the game.

Roland Hemond, who was a career baseballer himself and was married to the daughter of John Quinn, who had been head of the Philadelphia Phillies operation for many years, was ready to retire with a handshake. So Hemond was quick to join the cause, and he became encouragingly vocal in his support.

The cause, we consistently reported, was not only for the upper echelon of the game. It also included two other important elements—scouts and people in the Minor Leagues, including managers, coaches, and instructors. There were a few clubs that had patchwork pension plans. One club had a plan that only covered the owners and his relatives who worked in his organization. Every one of these few plans only covered some individuals as long as they remained with the parent club. Move on to another club and your benefits ended. And most of those benefits covered only a small percentage of the employees. I, however, was interested in covering as many people as possible.

80 }

Bowie had counseled that if I wanted to sell my idea for pensions for these forgotten souls of baseball, I would have to talk with all the Major League owners, since they were the ones who would have to vote yes or no on the proposal. With Bowie's advice in mind, I started out by meeting with pension and insurance people to develop some concepts of costs. I then tackled the owners. When I talked to the latter individually, virtually all agreed that it was an idea long overdue. The task proved to be long and detailed, but it was a satisfying one. Many owners had their financial people sit in on the presentations, and there was always a flock of questions, particularly about the economics of the plan.

Somehow the one visit that stands out in my mind was to the Chicago Cubs. William Wrigley III, the owner of the team and chewing gum magnate, met with me in his office in the Wrigley Building. He was one of the more influential owners in the game. I never addressed him as anything but "Mr. Wrigley." He allowed me a half hour to explain my case, and I did add that we were trying to get unanimous consent to start this new venture. His own response was succinct and to the point. "That sounds like a great idea, young man, and you can count on the Cubs to support it," he said as we parted.

The owners rebelled at funding past benefits, but apparently we flushed out all the other negatives. At the next joint meeting of the American and National leagues, the proposed new pension plan was approved unanimously. The plan covered all personnel from 1979 forward. At the outset, it provided for portability, so that benefits traveled with an individual moving from one club to another. If a scout worked eight years with the Baltimore Orioles and then went on to a better job with the Minnesota Twins, his eight years of benefits traveled with him. While we could not give veteran scouts and Minor League personnel credit for past benefits prior to 1979, the plan at least has covered them every year since, and the portability factor has been a great success.

While the World Series championships with the Orioles and Mets top my list of career high points, I am particularly proud of my role in helping to bring about a retirement plan for the non-playing people of baseball. An old friend, Harry Minor, who spent a highly successful career scouting for the Mets on the California coast, advised me to forget about mentioning "World Series" on my tombstone. "Put on there," he insisted, "that you finally got a pension for the little people in baseball. That's important!"

14

Baseball Trails

Although I hardly realized it along the way, my baseball journey brought me into contact with some great people, in and out of the game. You meet a truckload of interesting people along the baseball trail. One of my favorites was Emmett Ashford, the first African American umpire in the Major Leagues. Of persistent good humor, he regaled any listener with stories about his lengthy tribulations on his way through the Minor Leagues. "When I started out," he explained, "I understood there were going to be cracks about the color of my skin and I resolved not ever to let it affect my umpiring in calling the game."

I asked him then if he ever veered from that resolve. He paused a moment, smiled, and replied, "Well, maybe." Then, laughing all the way, he told me the following story.

"Once, in a Minor League game, I was calling the game at home plate. I made a simple call. I think it was ball four, and the young catcher in front of me turned around and asked me, 'Mr. Ashford, Mr. Ashford, could it be that Mr. Lincoln was wrong?' His remark stunned me and then something inside of me exploded and I threw him out of the game. He could have called me anything he wanted to, but bringing President Lincoln into it was the trigger that set me off."

Another favorite was Bart Giamatti, who resigned as president of Yale University to accept the job of commissioner of baseball in 1988. A scholarly executive who loved the game, he was well respected and loved at Yale, and I felt he would be similarly recognized in baseball. Even when he was at Yale, Giamatti wrote a lot about baseball. His almost lyrical writing showcased his intense love of the sport.

I had worked with colleges in various ways for a number of years and had been chairman of the board of Mount St. Mary's College in Emmitsburg, Maryland. So I tried to be helpful to Giamatti in his new assignment. Running baseball was not unlike heading a college, I promised him. The players, who were the backbone of the game, are not unlike students. The baseball office is the administration, not dissimilar to what you had in New Haven, I told him. As for the team owners, they are the equivalent of Yale's board of trustees. Bart and I had some lively personal discussions on these comparisons.

One thing that deeply impressed me was his quiet assertion that he didn't claim to have all the answers but was always open to advice. While still at Yale, Giamatti had frequently written {83 about baseball and in so doing revealed his love and respect for the game. When people ask me about baseball writing, I always direct them to Bart's work. His other reassuring move was to add Fay Vincent as his assistant. Fay was a lawyer who had held similar high-profile posts with national companies.

Unfortunately, Bart died of a heart attack at the age of fifty-one, only a year after becoming commissioner. It was a major loss for baseball. Giamatti had the potential to make a lasting impact on the game the way Branch Rickey did when he created the modern-day farm system and broke the color barrier with Jackie Robinson.

His assistant, Fay Vincent, was voted in as his successor and served three years before the baseball owners picked one of their own, Milwaukee Brewers owner Bud Selig, to be commissioner. Though his tenure was short, Vincent no doubt was influenced by Giamatti's fine mind, integrity, and love of the game.

Charlie Finley, the controversial owner of the Oakland Athletics, was another giant as a baseball executive who advanced the modern game. Described as a man who woke up with five new ideas every morning, Finley gets much of the credit for baseball's expansion in the 1960s and 1970s. That expansion brought Major League play to two-thirds of the country previously a baseball wasteland. Until the Dodgers and Giants moved to California in the late 1950s, the sixteen American and National League teams were clustered in the Northeast and Midwest and went only as far west and south as St. Louis and Washington DC.

Before the first westward expansion in 1958, New York City had three of those coveted MLB franchises—the storied Yankees, also known as the Bronx Bombers; the Brooklyn Dodgers, the beloved Bums of that famous borough; and the New York Giants of Polo Grounds fame. After World War II, there were anguished cries around the country for expansion and franchises in the West. As far as I know, the biggies who listened to those cries were, first of all, Horace Stoneham, who had signaled that he was going to take his New York Giants to San Francisco. As the story goes, Stoneham influenced his neighbor, Walter O'Malley, to move his Dodgers from one coast to the other. This, of course, set off a torrent of grief for Flatbush fans as the Dodgers set out for sunny Los Angeles, bringing joy to the West Coast and tears for New York, now down to a single Major League team.

84 }

At the time, television did not supply the big bucks it does today, and radio was still prime, but the hints of TV's potential were evident, and the countrywide sources of bigger and better dollars soon prevailed.

Expansion reached beyond country borders when a pair of major Canadian cities, Montreal and Toronto, got to the big leagues. That first surge dipped into Texas and several likely spots in the Midwest. Atlanta became a big league town in the mid-1960s, and combined with the addition of the two Texas cities of Houston and Dallas, this meant St. Louis was no longer the lone team close to the South.

Because of its location and wide broadcast network, St. Louis had finished first in the radio wars, if you can call the struggle for

1. My parents, Bridget and Cornelius Cashen.
(Courtesy of Cashen Family)

2. Sportswriting days at the *Baltimore News-Post*.
(Hearst Newspapers LLC/ *Baltimore News-American*)

3. Cashen and John Steadman, *Baltimore News-Post* sports editor.
(Courtesy of Baltimore Orioles)

4. Cashen (*left*) and O's owner Jerry Hoffberger (*second from left*); others unidentified. (Courtesy of Baltimore Orioles)

5. After '66 World Series sweep: (*from left*) manager Hank Bauer,
owner Jerry Hoffberger, general manager Frank Cashen.
(Courtesy of Baltimore Orioles)

6. Cashen with O's slugger Boog Powell. (Courtesy of Baltimore Orioles)

7. O's Hall of Fame pitcher Jim Palmer. (Courtesy of Baltimore Orioles)

8. Brooks Robinson—"he always excelled." (Courtesy of Baltimore Orioles)

9. "Friendly chat"—Earl Weaver and umpire. (Courtesy of Baltimore Orioles)

10. The Orioles' four twenty-game winners in 1970:
(*from left*) Dave McNally, Mike Cuellar, Jim Palmer, Pat Dobson.
(Courtesy of Baltimore Orioles)

11. Leading Baltimore's St. Patrick's Day Parade.
(Hearst Newspapers LLC/ *Baltimore News-American*)

12. Cashen (*right*) introducing Bob Hope in 1968.
(Hearst Newspapers LLC/*Baltimore News-American*)

13. Meeting President Nixon as Commissioner Bowie Kuhn (*center*) looks on.
(Hearst Newspapers LLC/*Baltimore News-American*)

14. Cashen, slugger Dave Kingman, and Mets manager Joe Torre, 1981.
(Courtesy of New York Mets)

15. Cashen with Mr. and Mrs. Ralph Kiner. (Courtesy of New York Mets)

16. Mets-wear: Frank in bow tie and hat. (Courtesy of New York Mets)

17. Cashen and Mets owner Nelson Doubleday.
(Courtesy of Flowerama Center, Ridgewood, New York)

18. "Tom Terrific"—pitching legend Tom Seaver. (Courtesy of New York Mets)

19. Lee Mazzilli—popular Met, unpopular trade.
(Courtesy of New York Mets)

20. Billy Beane during Mets playing days, 1981.
(Courtesy of New York Mets)

21. The Error Heard Round the World—Mets win sixth game after
Bill Buckner's error at first base. (Courtesy of New York Mets)

22. Shea Stadium: scene of my worst ('69) and best ('86) memories. (Courtesy of New York Mets)

23. '86 victory toast: (*from left*) Fred Wilpon, Nelson Doubleday, and Cashen. (Courtesy of Flowerama Center, Ridgewood, New York)

24. 1986 World Series trophy: Al Harazin, Joe McIlvanie, Cashen. (Courtesy of New York Mets)

25. New York ticker-tape parade after 1986 Series win: Frank and Jean Cashen in second car. (Source Unknown)

26. 2010 Mets Hall of Fame inductees:
(*from left*) Davey Johnson, Dwight Gooden, Darryl Strawberry,
and Cashen. (Courtesy of New York Mets)

JOHN FRANCIS "FRANK" CASHEN

GENERAL MANAGER & COO 1980-1991

HIS EYE FOR TALENT AND LEADERSHIP HELPED REVITALIZE A FRANCHISE THAT HAD FINISHED IN LAST PLACE FOR THREE CONSECUTIVE SEASONS...FROM 1984-1991, THE METS AVERAGED MORE THAN 95 VICTORIES EACH YEAR AND WON A WORLD SERIES CHAMPIONSHIP IN 1986 WITH A RECORD 108 WINS...WON 100 GAMES AND ANOTHER DIVISION TITLE TWO YEARS LATER...DRAFTED FUTURE ALL-STAR DARRYL STRAWBERRY AND TRADED FOR KEITH HERNANDEZ AND GARY CARTER.

   INDUCTED: 2010

27. Mets Hall of Fame plaque: John Francis "Frank" Cashen.
(Courtesy of Don Stukey)

28. Jean and Frank Cashen at their Maryland home.
(Photo by Karen Kyne Cashen)

29. Three generations of Cashens: (*first row seated, from left*) Stacey Effinger, Blaise Cashen, Jean Cashen, Frank Cashen, Gregory Cashen, Beverly Cashen, Karen Kyne Cashen; (*second row standing, from left*) Karen Krieger Cashen, Keely Cashen, Colby Cashen, Connor Effinger, Terry Cashen, Caitlin Cashen; (*third row standing, from left*) Seamus Cashen, Carly Cashen, Sean Cashen, Tim Cashen, Lucas Effinger, Brady Cashen, Scott Effinger, Dan Cashen, Brian Cashen. (Photo by Karen Kyne Cashen)

30. Frank with "Le Grand Orange"— Mets star Rusty Staub. (Courtesy of Chuck Solomon/*Sports Illustrated*)

31. Fay Vincent (*left*), then baseball commissioner, in golf cart with Frank Cashen. (Courtesy of New York Mets)

32. Frank Cashen throwing "first pitch" to catcher Gary Carter as wife Jean looks on. (Courtesy of New York Mets)

33. Frank with No. 41—"Tom Terrific" Seaver.
(Courtesy of New York Mets)

34. Frank and Mets manager Davey Johnson. (Courtesy of New York Mets)

35. Joe Torre, Mets manager, and Frank at spring training, 1981.
(Courtesy of New York Mets)

fans a war. When there was no competition west or south, the Cardinals had established firm radio networks in states hundreds of miles from St. Louis. During most of this time, the far-flung "Cardinal Nation" was blanketed by KMOX in St. Louis, a powerful 50,000-watt clear channel that permitted nighttime signals to be heard throughout much of the country. And they had solid announcers to call the games, starting with the audacious Dizzy Dean, who gave new meaning to the English language. The club followed with such stalwarts as Harry Caray and then Jack Buck.

Later, when I went with the Mets to Missouri to battle the Redbirds, Busch Stadium would be plastered in red—red caps, jerseys, banners, and signs. Many of those die-hard fans came from as far as three states away—Cardinals faithful who were converted by listening to radio broadcasts in the not-too-distant past. Those broadcasts were heard in Memphis by a young Elvis Presley and in Arkansas by a lad named Bill Clinton.   { 85

I remember the magic of radio broadcasts growing up in Baltimore, which, of course, had no Major League team at that time. I clearly remember being glued to an old Philco radio and listening to Arch McDonald doing play-by-play of the nearby Washington Senators baseball games. Gravel-voiced and almost stingy in what he had to offer, McDonald was my hero and for a long time thereafter the standard I used to judge future denizen of the craft.

Speaking of baseball expansion, Charlie Finley helped provide one of the most perplexing days of my career. At a meeting in Kansas City in 1968, the owners and general managers voted in the morning to move the Athletics out of that city to Oakland, allegedly because of the bad market in KC. Then, in the afternoon of the same day, we gave an expansion franchise to the same market, a team that was to be the Kansas City Royals. This strange turn of events occurred under pressure from Missouri's senior senator, Stuart Symington, who threatened lawsuits and legislation to revoke the league's antitrust exemption unless Kansas City got a replacement team in the Majors, and wealthy Kansas City pharmaceutical executive Ewing Kauffman became the owner of that expansion team.

Another celebrity I met during my years with the Mets was a future U.S. president, George W. Bush. As one of the owners of the Texas Rangers, George came to the baseball meetings, trailed by secret service agents because he was the son of then president George H. W. Bush. Many at the time thought the younger Bush would make a great baseball commissioner. If he had been offered that position, I think he would have snapped it up and never would have been governor of Texas, much less president of the United States.

Commissioner Bud Selig was always thinking about baseball when I first met him in Milwaukee. While I was still with the Orioles, I remember helping Bud put together a budget for his Milwaukee Brewers. A partner in a Jewish delicatessen, Bud always brought wonderful bagels to our get-togethers. Selig has had an up-and-down career as commissioner, but the bottom line is, attendance is up under his stewardship, overall salaries are way up, and some historic changes, such as the expanded playoffs and interleague play, have been made to improve the game.

Interleague play is popular with fans, has sharpened crosstown rivalries, as in New York and Chicago, and generally has increased attendance. The push for interleague play began before there was widespread national network and cable TV coverage of games from all over. By the time interleague play began in 1996, fans in one-league cities already had access to TV coverage of games from both leagues. Before that time, I had often said, for instance, "It would be a shame if folks in the National League city of Atlanta never got to see the Orioles' Brooks Robinson play."

One reason the great Stan Musial was underappreciated in many parts of the country was because the Cardinal star played before the era of national TV coverage. Fans in American League cities never saw him play because the Cardinals had a World

Series drought between 1946, before TV coverage, and 1964, by which time Musial had retired. Stan played in four World Series, all in the 1940s before national TV coverage of the Fall Classic.

Although talked about during my time in the commissioner's office, interleague play would not join the MLB scene for another sixteen years. As administrator of baseball, Commissioner Kuhn had fed me a series of responsible assignments in the late 1970s. Since I knew most of the general managers personally from my years at Baltimore, things went well and I was happy in the job. So I was somewhat surprised when the Commish told me he had received a phone call from a newly purchased franchise that was interested in talking to me about running their club. That club, of course, was the New York Mets.

15

Casting My Fate

The Paysons, one of New York's elite families, were the owners of the Mets since the team's inception as an expansion franchise in the early 1960s. The Paysons' decision to sell had brought some serious bidding, and the club was ultimately purchased by a group led by Fred Wilpon, a real estate developer. The group featured Nelson Doubleday and his massive publishing empire as the dominant member. The price was $21 million, which at the time was the highest price ever paid for a baseball team and more than twice what George Steinbrenner's consortium had paid for the New York Yankees a few years earlier. The sale history shows that the second-highest bidder had offered $19 million, and there were several other offers at slightly lesser amounts.

Gossip has it that when his group was in conflict over what to offer for the Mets, Doubleday had suggested $21 million, citing the well-known restaurant frequented by the New York sports set. This was, of course, "21."

Two thoughts immediately came to mind as I considered the possibility of working with the Mets and their new owners. In the commissioner's office, I missed the challenge of winning or losing every day through the 162-game season. Working at headquarters was safe and rewarding, but I did miss the competitive part of the sport. The second thought was, in fact, a negative one. The Mets had finished last or next to last for five straight seasons. The previous year the team had sold fewer than 800,000 tickets, a pitiful mark. It was not unfair to call them the worst team in baseball.

Presale media comments described the Mets' Minor League operations as devoid of talent and virtually worthless. To me, the whole situation appeared impossible. What a challenge! Nothing ventured, nothing gained. I agreed to talk with the new owners. Several of the would-be partners Wilpon had lined up started to drop out, and Doubleday picked up their shares. He was now the principal owner. He was the man to see, and I went to see him.

An affable, large-sized gent, Doubleday and I hit it off immediately. The first question I asked him was "Do you expect to make money out of this investment?" He replied that he didn't expect to make money right away but he thought that eventually he would. That was the perfect answer so far as I was concerned. First, there would be time to build, and second, I was not interested in working for a nonprofit organization.

Nelson Doubleday Jr. was the third generation of his family to head the book publishing company his grandfather started. At one time it was the largest publisher in the United States. After college, Nelson started in the family business as a copywriter and worked his way up through the organization, becoming president in 1978. Among his other activities, Nelson was a dedicated and accomplished golfer, a member of seven of the top golf courses in the country and a regular in the Concours d'Elegance, an annual celebration at Pebble Beach, California, where the captains of industry got together with the show business crowd.

Doubleday also had a fine working appreciation of good wines, a cellar full of ancient sherry, and a personal preference for a good Italian white, which appeared at every luncheon table where he dined. For health reasons, Nelson finally gave up all versions of alcohol, and I had every reason to go into mourning. He and I had some great sessions together, and it was after a couple of the earlier meetings in 1980 that I decided to accept the offer to run the Mets.

During those discussions, I remember a searching question he asked: "Frank, if you accepted our offer, how long would it take you to turn this team around?" That was a question I had asked myself more than once in the past weeks. I quickly shot back, "Four or five years." When Nelson didn't flinch, I moved closer to taking the job. I guess the size of the challenge finally induced me to say yes, and sometime in mid-February 1980, we agreed on a deal.

Fred Wilpon, now a minority stockholder, sat in on most of the proceedings, and it was evident to me that he wanted some part of the administration. Nelson told me Fred would be listed as club president early on, but in two years, after I had straightened out the baseball side to his satisfaction, I would assume the role of president in addition to that of general manager. It was hectic for a while after I accepted the new position. Wrapping up the job in the commissioner's office and vacating my office and moving from midtown Manhattan to Shea Stadium in Queens took some doing.

A press conference to announce my appointment with the Mets was the first order of business, and that went smoothly. I remember I was wearing a bow tie at the introductory gathering, a habit I had developed long before in the newspaper business, where I had labored for so many years. There, you were frequently called upstairs to the composing room, almost a daily visit to check on one's story, usually slated for the next edition. Early on, I learned that when you leaned over the fresh pages of cold lead type being "made up" you inadvertently got a bar of printer's ink across a long tie, thus ruining it for future use. Some of the old-timers had suggested that bow ties took care of the problem. Always ready to learn from more experienced teachers, I started wearing bow ties to work but kept a healthy supply of long ties for social activities and the like.

Somehow the bow tie had been especially noticed at the Mets' press conference. When I attended the next public event in a traditional long tie, the press asked about the absence of my bow tie and seemed disappointed by its disappearance. I made a decision right then that if bow ties were to be seen as my trademark, so be it. My small collection at the time then grew exponentially. Bill Torrey, the GM and COO of the then hockey champion Long Island Islanders, and an executive I much admired, had already been labeled by his short neckwear. So I was comfortable in joining such worthwhile company.

Another interesting incident took place while I was moving my personal papers into the new Shea Stadium office. (Completed in 1964 to house the expansion-team Mets, the stadium was, in my opinion, correctly named after Bill Shea, a prominent New York lawyer. Shea had led the fight to bring a National League team back to New York after the Dodgers and Giants had absconded to California in 1958.)

As I wrestled with a small collection of personal boxes, I suddenly realized that the adjoining office was also being outfitted and that Wilpon was directing the proceedings. I took him aside quickly and asked what was going on. He replied that, as president of the club, he was establishing a working office at Shea. I told him I thought it was a terrible idea, and that under the terms of my contract I was to have complete control of the ball park and that his presence around the office would undermine my responsibilities. I added that I felt anyone who would be contacting the Mets for any reason, and not knowing the working parts of the organization, would seek out the president rather than the VP, and that was not the way we had set things up.

To emphasize the point, I asked him if he had discussed his intentions with Nelson. He never really answered, assuring me instead he would be no bother to me. I answered that if he stayed, I was going back to my old job. That was how strongly I felt about the matter. Fred changed his tune and was very gracious. He said he had no intention of upsetting me and that he had changed his mind on the spot and would be vacating the premises immediately. We never discussed the matter again, and from then on Fred and I had a smooth relationship throughout my long tenure with the Mets.

{ 91

The fact is that in 1980 Wilpon had less than 5 percent of the club. Nelson Doubleday was by far the dominant owner. City Investment, another owner, had a relatively smaller share than Doubleday and, within a short time, sold out to him. Although he was kept informed as to what was going on, Fred had little to say about the club at that time. Then in 1986 he came up with half interest with Doubleday and, of course, after 2002 he became sole owner of the franchise.

With the internal administration details worked out, I turned my attention to the baseball side. I was not optimistic. Knowing the franchise was about to change hands, the administration did little or nothing to the outfit that finished last in the National League East the previous year. It was now late February and the team was already in spring training in St. Petersburg, on Florida's Gulf Coast.

The weakness of the previous administration was well known to me. I had worked with the Mets in a significant deal some years earlier, so I had firsthand experience. It all happened at the winter meetings in 1975, my last year with the Orioles. Ever trying to improve my club, I had been looking for another veteran hitter. I approached the Mets about trading Rusty Staub, whom I had admired for several seasons but who was languishing with the "going nowhere" Mets. The New York club had been seeking a third baseman for years, and the Orioles had a couple of good young prospects who could fill the bill. The centerpiece of the discussion was Doug DeCinces, who was full of promise as a Minor Leaguer and went on to become a standout infielder in the Majors. Joe McDonald, a good baseball man who was negotiating for the other side, wanted something in addition, so the Orioles put another promising Minor Leaguer into the discussion. He certainly was not of the caliber of DeCinces. Not surprisingly, the Mets management appeared to be satisfied with the deal.

The reason for the Orioles' largess at third was the presence of Brooks Robinson, a future Hall of Famer, at third base. At age thirty-eight, Brooks showed no sign of being even close to retirement. This was a good example of one of my theories about trading players: if you can trade from your strength and shore up your weaknesses, it's the way to go. Joe McDonald said that Donald Grant, the Wall Street heavy who was running his Mets club, had approved the deal. He asked that we wait until the following morning to make the announcement so he could brief Mrs. Lorinda de Roulet, the current Mets owner and a daughter of the Payson family, who was due in that evening. Of course we agreed, but that night we informed our people of the particulars and counseled them to keep the matter under their hats until the announcement was made the next morning.

After a sound night's sleep, convinced I had helped the Orioles, I was up early the next morning and grabbed an elevator on my way to the hotel coffee shop. An old, good friend and fellow GM, Roland Hemmond, was in the same elevator and asked what I thought of the deal the Mets had made last night. Fearing the New Yorkers had made the announcement without me, I feigned surprise only to be told that the Mets had traded Rusty Staub to the Detroit Tigers for veteran left-hand pitcher Mickey Lolich, who I felt was far past his prime. I hurried to find McDonald, who told me sheepishly that Mrs. De Roulet felt they shouldn't trade Rusty for rookie players. He was ordered to go to his second option, which was the veteran Detroit lefty. He had made the deal that very night, and since some of the sportswriters were aware of the trade as it was in the works, an announcement had been made immediately.

As you can imagine, I was bitterly disappointed both in losing Rusty and in the shoddy way the Mets handled the matter. Ironically, I signed Staub six years later, as a free agent, for his second stint with the Mets, and he made a significant contribution as we built toward the 1986 World Series win. Once you looked at Rusty Staub and saw that flaming red head of hair, you would never forget his name; the rusty part was a natural.

Long before I had ever seen him play, I was interested in young Mr. Staub. He was a schoolboy out of New Orleans when he first gained notice in baseball. A graduate of a New Orleans Jesuit high school, Rusty was signed by the Major League expansion franchise Houston Colts in 1961. It is fair to say he was rushed to the big leagues, and at age nineteen he was the Houston first baseman and his daily performances were followed by the national press.

Rusty played, and played well, with five teams in the Majors for twenty-three years. He should be in baseball's Hall of Fame in Cooperstown, but he keeps being passed over as younger sportswriters participate in the annual voting. Staub's offensive figures (292 career home runs and just 284 hits shy of the magic 3,000 milestone) are better than over half the players already in the Hall. Nevertheless, he doesn't get the votes, and his ever-declining chances are quickly reaching zero.

I confess Rusty was my kind of player. In short, he was tougher in pressure situations. For instance, if a much-needed run was at third base with either no outs or one out, I would rather have Rusty coming to bat than any ballplayer I knew. He would get that run home. You could count on it. When we needed a sacrifice fly or run-scoring hit, you could watch Le Grand Orange, a title he picked up while playing in Canada, choke up on the bat, shorten his batting stance, and produce the RBI.

Following his New Orleans heritage, Rusty had a great talent with food. He was a wonderful chef and a first-class restaurateur. In two different locations in the heart of New York City, he produced first-class eating. No wonder I consider him special.

Rusty has another special talent, and as he has grown older, it has become an all-consuming obsession: wine. With baseball and restaurants behind him, he devotes most of his day to the wine business, his principal means of support in selling wine he has gathered from California vineyards or from growers in France and other countries. That has necessitated frequent travels abroad to gather those valued cases he sells to world-class restaurants and to well-heeled individual collectors.

So, in addition to the Mets' woeful on-field performance in the years before 1980, I was joining a club that had a recent history of ineffectual front-office management. With the new owners in charge, I felt reassured that I could make the changes needed to make the Mets a winner.

16

Changing the Mets' Image

If there was anything I had to change immediately upon taking over the Mets, it was my own negative impressions of the franchise. The Mets had beaten Baltimore in the 1969 World Series, when I believed the O's had a superior team. Baltimore was back in the league playoffs the following two years while the Mets fell back to also-rans, and the Rusty Staub debacle in 1975 had done nothing to change my mind.

One hole was evident in the Mets' administrative staff that we inherited in the early spring of 1980, and it was apparent immediately. There was a public relations director on the job, but no one to handle the press on a day-to-day basis. Like so many other things, it was the wrong time of year to be trying to fill that spot. Two names were suggested to me. The first was Joe Black, who held a similar job with the National Football League. After a personal visit and conversation, it was apparent Joe had no interest in leaving football. That left me with just one person who had shown interest. That was Jay Horwitz, a New Jerseyite who managed public relations at nearby Farleigh Dickinson University.

Frankly, Jay did not interview well and seemed to be generally discombobulated. He even spilled a glass of orange juice on me as we talked. But I discerned a positive note in his enthusiasm for the slot, so I decided to give him a try. I persuaded myself I had no other choice, and the field would be wide open in a couple of months. That was early in 1980, and although I felt he made some serious mistakes those first years, overall his performance advanced the Mets' image. Jay is still working for the Mets today and is looked upon as one of the best in the business. It certainly wasn't apparent when he started out.

As for the ball club, Joe Torre was the manager, with former Cardinals great Bob Gibson as his pitching coach—in my opinion the second most important job on the team. I knew Torre was an excellent ballplayer who had been named player-manager three years earlier. He had dropped the player part after a few weeks. By coincidence, Joe's father, an ex–New York City detective, had earlier worked as an assistant scout for the Baltimore Orioles. Gibson was, of course, equally well known in baseball as an outstanding pitcher for the St. Louis Cardinals in a career that ultimately sent him to the Hall of Fame in Cooperstown.

Certainly then, I figured the club was in good hands. It was already too late for me to do anything about it anyway, and I so advised owner Nelson Doubleday. I would spend the 1980 season re-evaluating the team, getting to know the farm system, the scouting system, and the Shea Stadium personnel. It didn't take long for me to be convinced that the Mets were as bad as I had imagined. John Stearns, the catcher, may have been as close to a Major Leaguer as we had. He was our constant contribution to the annual All-Star Games. And that, perhaps, was because the rules demanded at least one player be selected from each club. Lee Mazzilli was another Met with more than average ability. He was a switch-hitting outfielder with good defensive skills. But more on him later.

Both at home and on the road, I kept copious notes. In post-game visits to the clubhouse, I found Torre stoically silent, staring into his locker, and he appeared to have no idea about how to improve things. That was not totally surprising, since he had little in the way of talent with which to work. Neither did Gibson, who was attempting to teach lesser-talented hurlers to mimic him. No chance.

It was not until sometime in the 1981 season that I began to think about making a change in the manager and his coaches. But

{ 97

the notes also show that it would have served no purpose to make such moves in the middle of things. Midseason moves are usually chancy at best. Such changes of the guard work when you have someone in your own system to step into the job. For example, in Baltimore, Earl Weaver, then a Major League coach, was ready when we let Hank Bauer go back in 1968. Circumstances with the Mets were different, and with no heir apparent it made more sense to wait until the end of the baseball season when the list of potential candidates would be considerably larger. Then, too, the team was floundering badly, and a mere change of managers was not going to do much to alleviate that condition. I waited for the end of that season before beginning to make wholesale changes.

On the team-building front, let it be known I was always a firm believer in scouts, and had worked with some of the best of them, as you will read. They found and fingered the amateur talent and brought it to the club. Baseball teams can have great managers and coaches in the Minors, but it's ultimately the talent you trust them with that is most important. Scouts, like everyone else in life, come with different gifts. The ability to evaluate the evaluators is one of the basic duties of the general manager. In fact, evaluating the evaluators and having the courage of your own convictions are, to me, the most important attributes for a GM. Listen to your people, welcome their opinions, seek their ideas, but, in the end, the ultimate decisions come down to the GM. The GM makes that final call.

Having finished last in 1980, the Mets had first pick in the June free agent draft. Three months in, I had scant opportunity to evaluate our evaluators, so I picked out a couple of veteran scouts and went along with their selections.

One thing was evident but not totally surprising: there was good high school talent in Southern California. Some of our scouts favored Darryl Strawberry, an outfielder from the Watts section of Los Angeles. Straw had college scholarship offers for basketball as well as baseball. At six feet five, he was a first-class prospect in both sports, a fact already noted in a *Sports Illustrated* magazine story.

Some of our other talent evaluators preferred Billy Beane, an outfielder from San Diego who already was offered a free ride to Stanford, where he was promised a slot as their football quarterback. He was said to be a very intelligent as well as athletically talented young man. The other young talent was John Gibbons, a high school catcher from Texas. These three became our first picks in the June lottery. The draft was not completely new to me, since I had been through it ten times with the Orioles. But this was different, since the underpinnings of that club were more solid and I had only to rubber-stamp what the scouting department recommended.

Strawberry, of course, proved to be one of the most successful Mets players in history. The other two, Beane and Gibbons, reached their peaks eventually with other organizations. As mentioned previously, Beane turned to administration and became the longtime general manager of the Oakland Athletics. John Gibbons developed into a Major League manager, piloting the Toronto Blue Jays.

When the Orioles had perennial powerhouse teams, we'd ask our scouts an additional question: "Is he a potential Orioles player?" We were forever trying to judge whether a youngster was going to be just a good player or a winning player, an Orioles player. Two titans I recall from those dominant Baltimore years were two scouts. Bill Werl was our number one sleuth in the American League from his home in Oakland, California. A former left-handed Major League pitcher, he was an excellent student of that skill and a pretty good judge of baseball talent in general. Actually, Bill worked double duty. Besides his permanent Major League assignment, we sent Bill to scout the top free-agent high school and college pitchers and rate them from one to ten. When draft day came, we would select them, if they were still in the overall draft, exactly according to Bill's preferences.

Jim Russo, whom I later labeled "Super Scout," was our man in the National League. He lived and worked out of St. Louis and was remarkable. Early on, he was brilliant in free agent sweepstakes and signed such players as Jim Palmer, Dave McNally, and Davey Johnson. Now concentrating on the National League, he was the front man on swaps that had brought the Orioles Mike Cuellar and Pat Dobson.

Here is a truism that I uncovered—at least uncovered to my own satisfaction: There are ballplayers you win with and ballplayers you lose with—and it doesn't always depend on batting average or earned run averages.

Having had experience in both baseball and horse racing, I was amazed how similar they could be. When you had a good young horse, you were constantly trying to divine what he had inside. Did he have heart? It was the same with a young ballplayer. What kind of heart did he have? Was he going to be a winner?

100 }

In my book, usually the best free agent draft you can make is a college pitcher. And the riskiest, a high school pitcher. With the college pitcher, you have two or three years more on his arm; and in two or three additional years, he could well be on your Major League staff. A seventeen-year-old high school hurler is five or, maybe, even six years away from the bigs, and a lot can happen to a young arm during that waiting period. One thing more, my theory, for some unexplained reason, is that left-handed pitching takes a lot longer to develop than right-handed. Many baseball people would not agree on that point, but I have had a lot of success with my own thinking, another example of having the courage of one's convictions. Having had a resounding respect for left-handed throwers on the mound, early in my career I described it this way: "Left-handed pitching is like sex—you never seem to get enough of either." Perhaps it was a flip remark, but it caught the attention of a few and was repeatedly repeated.

I have always felt it was good to have a potential Major League manager in a Minor League system. It was good to have somebody honing his skills down below; in short, learning to manage, learning from his mistakes, learning which moves work and which don't.

Few, if any, individuals can step from being a player to being a Major League skipper. I feel that time in the Minor Leagues is a must. I was lucky when I took over the Orioles. They already had Earl Weaver as a Minor League manager, and he had worked at virtually every level of the Minor League system.

After I had taken over the Mets, I wanted to groom a future manager from their Minor League system. It was about then that Davey Johnson came to me looking for a managing job. Johnson had played second base for the Orioles and I had traded him to Atlanta for catcher Earl Williams in what was one of the worst trades of my career. An intelligent young man who had a degree in mathematics from a Texas college, Johnson had managerial potential. I felt that with a little experience he could be a good manager, so I offered him a slot in the Minors. He quickly found success there and after a couple years, in late 1983, I reached out to hire him to manage the Mets.

17

Yellow Pad Parlance

In my bottom desk drawer, I kept a yellow legal pad with a collection of my personal baseball beliefs written down. Among these was a notation about the ten things to look for in a Major League manager, and also an ever-changing list of individuals I would want to interview if we needed a big league skipper. As to the former, the list of qualities you should seek in a manager,

I had accumulated that over time. It consisted of ten items—five above an imaginary line, and five below the line.

The above-line group had to do with the actual playing of the game, and they were the most important. The below-the-line items had mostly to do with off-the-field qualities. One that has arisen in recent years is the ability to get along with the owners. The owners used to buy a ball club, hire veteran baseball personnel to run it, and then stay out of the way. Today, a lot of owners want to have a close one-on-one relationship with the manager, which often leads to disappointment for one side or the other.

The list itself had the same ten slots from the beginning, but occasionally I moved an item from the top to the bottom and vice-versa. When I first got into baseball, we ruled from what I called the fear syndrome: "This is the way we do things and this is the way you will do them or you will be buried in the Minor Leagues forever." With the advent of agents, free agency, and the strides made by the players' union, such a policy was no longer feasible. The arrival of so many players from so many other countries in Latin America and Asia contributed to the reality.

The reality had changed the number one item above the line to "The ability to understand, get along with, and communicate with your twenty-five-man active squad." An example of the below-the-line group was the ability to represent the team well in off-field matters, such as press conferences.

My fellow general managers knew of my yellow pad guidelines. If they were particularly good friends, it was not uncommon for them to phone and ask me for suggestions when seeking to fill spots on their own teams. Fortunately, those conversations were never revealed to the media. One exception resulted from a call I got from my friend John McHale of the Montreal Expos. He explained that his son, John Jr., had taken over the Colorado Rockies expansion franchise. He needed a manager. Knowing that John Sr. was a very good friend of mine, John Jr. had asked his father to contact me about his interest in hiring Don Baylor, who had grown up in the Orioles organization. He wanted my thoughts on the matter.

{ 103

I immediately responded that if ever I were in a foxhole and my life depended on it, the people I would want to be there with me were Don Shula and Don Baylor. Shula would figure out how we were going to get out and Baylor would be the first guy over the top, leading us. Shula, of course, was the legendary Miami Dolphins coach and a family friend from his days with the Baltimore Colts. The senior McHale must have repeated my advice to his son, and it was quoted several times before making its way into the press. Oh, yes, Baylor got the job, and under his managership in the 1990s, the Rockies had the best five-year record of any MLB expansion club ever.

But here I was, still figuring out the Mets. In my final meeting with Joe Torre, I explained to him that if I was going to rebuild the Mets, I would have to start getting my own people into key spots within the organization. I assured him he would have other opportunities to manage and would need more experience. Try the Minors, I suggested. He did not appear to welcome that advice and, understandably, was unhappy with being terminated. And the fact that Joe and his older brother, Frank, a veteran first baseman who had played with the Braves and Phillies, were native New Yorkers, didn't make the separation from the Mets any easier for Joe or me.

Joe's brother Frank and I remained close friends. Frank had been a Major League first baseman and we talked baseball by the hour. We also played a lot of golf tournaments.

After several attempts at managing, Joe was off the field for some time and became a color commentator on radio and TV for Gene Autry's California Angels. Autry told me that Torre was doing a great job in the broadcast booth and seemed to have happily settled in Southern California. Joe's wife was a neat lady, and she and Joe had a lovely daughter. Southern California seemed to be the perfect spot for them.

104 }   In late 1995 I got a call from Frank, who explained that Joe had asked him to call me. Joe was toying with an offer from George Steinbrenner to come back to New York and manage the struggling Yankees. He wasn't quite sure what to do and asked his brother to quietly get my thoughts on the subject. I was surprised to get the call and I remember telling Frank that I would not and, truthfully, could not give him an immediate answer. I said I'd call him back in the morning.

It was back to the old yellow pad exercise. I looked at the matter from every conceivable angle, and midmorning the following day I called Frank. My advice was to tell Joe to stay where he was in Los Angeles. He had a good job with the Angels, was well liked, his family was happy, and Southern California was a great place to raise a family. Besides, I cautioned, if the team didn't improve dramatically the first year, Steinbrenner would blame him. George at this time was firing managers at a record clip, and going back to manage in New York would be no walk in Central Park. That was the best advice I could give and I stood by it. Fortunately, Joe Torre didn't pay any attention to me, went

back to New York, and had a storybook run with the Yankees
for twelve years. I have often thought that Torre did more for
Steinbrenner than Steinbrenner did for Torre.

As for the Mets in 1981, I didn't have a load of options. The
Minor League department had made some progress, but the
Major League club was still lacking everywhere. There was no
quick fix, and it became even more apparent that any rebuilding
would have to be from the ground up. Selecting a new manager
was the first task. There was no one in the organization worth
taking a chance on. Maybe just as important, you can't win in the
big leagues without good pitching; in fact, you can't win in any
league without good pitching. It is 65 percent of the game, I had
previously stated. That thought came flooding back.

The previous season had not been a complete waste. We produced a good amateur draft and I had time to figure out what
it was going to take to turn the team around. I went looking for {105
good teachers to add to my coaching staff, but most of all, we
were going to have to come up with pitching from somewhere.
My theory is that you had to add another starting pitcher to your
staff every two years. If it wasn't from your farm system, it had to
come from somewhere. Trade! Just as with players, it can take a
few seasons for a young manager to transition up to the Majors.
And most of them still have a lot to learn when they get there.
On-the-job coaching in the Majors continues their education.

With all this in mind, my thoughts went outside the Mets
organization. I remembered George Bamberger, who had been
the pitching coach for the Baltimore Orioles the last eight years
I was there. I considered him to be the best in the business. He
combined discipline with marvelous teaching skills and a great
grasp of the craft. His efforts had brought the Orioles those four
twenty-game winners (Mike Cuellar, Pat Dobson, Dave McNally,
and Jim Palmer) in the 1970s and a solid pitching ensemble every
year. Bamberger had a unique philosophy of pitching. He believed
that the arm, a series of muscles, should be exercised every day

and starting pitchers should start every fourth day. He also believed they should be ready to go nine innings at each outing. Having witnessed George's success closely for eight seasons, I was an advocate of his methods and still am.

I confess I don't know who came up with the new thinking that starting pitchers only have to go four or five innings and then you go to someone who is said to be a "long relief" pitcher. After the latter is through, there is a short reliever, followed by a lead-up, then to a so-called closer. The combination never seemed to me as impressive as an old-time starter who could go the distance. After I left the Orioles, Harry Dalton, who had known Bambi years before I did, later recruited him to manage the Milwaukee Brewers, the first of two separate managerial stints in the Wisconsin city.

But Bambi was not working for anybody in 1982, having sat out the 1981 season. From the moment I first contacted him at his Florida home and told him I was interested in his managing the team, we spent the bulk of the time talking pitching. There is no chance we can win, or even come close to it, in the next two years, I confessed. But, I said, we have to make strides in that direction. "I'll get you some pitching prospects," I promised, "and I need you to nurture them into Major League winners." As I remember, George asked me, "What the hell do you mean by nurture?" After a few more phone calls to talk about salary and fringe benefits, Bambi agreed to manage the Mets.

Hiring Bamberger, I thought, was a big step in the right direction, although the New York press didn't see it that way. "Why didn't you get Earl Weaver?" was the most often asked question. That exercise was the first step in solving a puzzle that took me a couple years to understand.

In places like Baltimore, from my personal experience, but also in markets such as Minnesota, Cincinnati, and Atlanta, a GM could take over a team of losers and promise that it would take a few years to build a winner. The fans in those cities would take you at your word and wait patiently and faithfully follow and support the team in the interim. Not so in New York. Even with the reputation of being the best and most knowledgeable fans in the country, they want to know why you don't have a winner this year. Maybe you can stretch that to two years, but not five. New York fans care little about what you have in your Triple-A team, the next step to the Majors, or what kind of draft you accomplished at the lowest level. They want to know who is going to play center field for the Mets this season. New York is a center-field town. That's where Joe DiMaggio, Mickey Mantle, Willie Mays, and Duke Snider played.

In Bamberger's first year, we brought up a couple of good prospects from our depleted farm system. These included William Hayward Wilson, better known as Mookie Wilson, a speedy outfielder from South Carolina, and Hubie Brooks, a California third baseman. Both helped greatly in the early days of the rebuilding process. Another player of note was Ron Gardenhire, an infielder who got some playing time at the Major League level, but who ultimately went on to coach and later to successfully manage the Minnesota Twins. Neil Allen, a stocky right-handed fireballer, was a dependable relief pitcher who showed promise for the future.

But the natives were restless, as we will see in the pages ahead. Despite these gradual improvements to the team, fans were hungry for a winner . . . and soon.

18

Trade Secrets

As expected, we limped through Bamberger's first season as manager in 1982 and barely merited any headlines, although I did my best to notify every franchise that the Mets were interested in trading ballplayers. It was disappointing but hardly unexpected to find out that we had little to offer in the trade department. However, in spite of the rash of bad news, I did pull off what I consider was the key trade in rebuilding the Mets. Knowing we were slim in the pitching department and remembering my promise to Bamberger, I was looking for promising Minor League pitchers. I worked out a deal with Texas Rangers GM Eddie Robinson, who was looking for a left-handed power-hitting outfielder. We had Lee Mazzilli, a switch hitter best from the left side and a native New Yorker, who was the fan favorite on the Mets.

I knew it was going to be a vastly unpopular move, but I swapped him to Texas for a pair of promising, young right-hand pitchers—Ron Darling and Walt Terrell. Darling, a Yale graduate who then was better known for his academic feats than his physical prowess, lived up to his promise. He was a Met mainstay for many years, including that ultimate World Series victory over the Boston Red Sox in 1986. Terrell was no disappointment either. I had pictured both youngsters as starting pitchers for us when we had built our club into contenders. But as we were on that path, we got into a discussion with Detroit management and traded Terrell to the Tigers for their highly rated young third baseman, Howard Johnson. Our scouts were right. Ho Jo was a major contributor to the club for many years with his bat, with his glove at third, and, ultimately, as a Minor League manager and Major League hitting coach with the Mets. The Mazzilli trade drew a rash of negative fan mail as well as encounters on the street. Two of those incidents still stand out in my mind. One sunny afternoon in late fall, my wife, Jean, and I were walking down New York's Fifth Avenue when a car screeched to a stop near the curb just in front of us. An angry young man jumped out and took up a belligerent position facing us. "Why the hell did you ever trade Mazzilli?" he demanded, as an inquisitive crowd started to gather. I don't remember what I stammered in reply, but after making a few more remarks about my lack of all mental capacity, he jumped back in the car and disappeared. Jean handled the matter in good humor and joined the crowd in a quiet laugh. Although I was getting used to similar queries, I didn't laugh but just walked away and continued my window shopping at Saks.

{ 109

I well remember one other incident. First let me explain that if in midday we had to go into Manhattan from our office at Shea Stadium in Queens, the fastest way was to take the No. 7 subway. A subway stop was located not more than two city blocks from our office door. A twenty-minute ride to Grand Central Station, that subway route was popular and usually well traveled, as it was on the day in question. I jumped aboard and took a seat in one of the forward and more crowded cars.

No sooner had I sat down than I noticed a gentleman sitting directly opposite staring at me intensely. It was evident that he was trying to figure out who I was, but he was looking directly at my bow tie. His gaze brightened as he must have put together the bow tie, plus where I had gotten on the train. Pointing an accusatory finger, he proclaimed in a voice that bordered on a shout, "Frank Cashen, why in the name of God did you ever trade Lee Mazzilli?" The whole car appeared to be leaning forward, awaiting the answer. I just smiled and tried to sink out of sight in the subway seat. The rest of that year, and all of the next, when

I used the No. 7 line, I untied my bow and hid it in my pocket before venturing onto the train.

The Mazzilli trade was, of course, a step for the future. I tried a few other moves to shore up the club. Not that they were all that successful, but they did partially take the pressure off the real building process. (Mazzilli returned to the Mets in 1986, helped us in the World Series that year, but never achieved the level of performance of his first stint and retired after the 1989 season.)

Going back a bit, a sidebar adventure in my life led to a major negotiation as the Mets GM. In 1979, while working for the commissioner's office, I was sent to Japan to lead a National League all-star team headed by LA Dodgers manager Tommy Lasorda, to take on an American League all-star team, under the irascible Earl Weaver himself. Pittsburgh Pirates manager Chuck Tanner was Lasorda's assistant, and Orioles first base coach Jim Frey backed up Weaver. Both assistants became more important as the tour unfolded.

Weaver was "overserved" in the lounge at JFK Airport as we gathered for the flight to Japan. I knew, with some degree of certainty, that my troubles were just starting and would continue throughout the trip. We were still in the airport when I spoke with Frey, who was a good friend from our Oriole days, and asked him to keep a close watch on Weaver and be prepared to step in to run the team if Earl stumbled. Frey, who had served as a coach under Weaver and knew better than I the possible pitfalls ahead, reluctantly agreed. It was apparent that he was not happy with the assignment. Looking for a descriptive word, I would say that Weaver and Frey struggled through the trip.

As part of the tour, the commissioner had arranged to have two of the games telecast on ESPN back to the United States, with the two managers taking turns as lead announcers. To my mind, it would be too risky to put Weaver on a national TV program and I so advised the ESPN people, who agreed with me.

Lasorda and his henchmen did an extraordinary job on TV. With a very simple trick, Tommy would turn the team over to Tanner.

Before he climbed to the broadcast booth, the pair would discuss the operating signals for the team: when to use the sacrifice bunt, the hit-and-run, the take sign for the batter, and so on. So when Tanner put on the signal for the bunt, in the broadcast booth Lasorda would proclaim, "This is a perfect time for a sacrifice bunt." When the maneuver followed, he praised the way Tanner ran the team. And, of course, the ESPN listeners across the country were silently praising Lasorda for being such a knowledgeable baseball man.

We substituted Tanner for the lead announcer in the second matchup. With Tanner calling the plays up in the press box, Lasorda, of course, went back to managing the team. Since they again discussed the signs before the game, Tanner described Lasorda as a virtual genius as he followed the prescribed signals. Weaver got through the rest of the trip and remained the consummate baseball manager for years thereafter. Frey, another lifetime base-baller, went on to manage the Kansas City Royals and the Chicago Cubs and later was the Cubs' GM. In between his managerial jobs, Frey was a coach for the Mets in 1982 and '83 and one of the best hitting tutors I've ever seen. He was seriously underestimated for the part he played in making a young Darryl Strawberry an all-star hitter at an early age.

Although I had already spent ten years with the Orioles, I had little firsthand knowledge of the National League. Reading the scouting reports and checking the daily box scores, I had a general idea about who were the leading batters and best pitchers. But the all-star trip to Japan gave me an opportunity to see them all—well, maybe most of them—firsthand. For me, the best of them was the St. Louis Cardinals' switch-hitting catcher, Ted Simmons. Lasorda penciled him in as the cleanup hitter in virtually every game played by that all-star squad.

Another slugger who caught my eye was George Foster, the Cincinnati Reds' left fielder, who at this time was a free agent. He had tremendous power, and when I later had a chance to sign him for the Mets I leaped at it. When I met with Foster's agent in Sarasota, Florida, it quickly became apparent that we were talking about significant dollars, like a $1 million signing bonus and a five-year deal starting at $1 million-plus the first year and annual increases through the remainder of the agreement.

When I conveyed this news to Nelson Doubleday, he did not blink even though this was big money for a baseball contract in the early 1980s. Apparently, this kind of money was not unknown in the publishing business. Doubleday then introduced me to the concept of deferred compensation. In such an arrangement, the publishing house and the writer would agree on an initial payment and future dollars over a specified period of time. The writer might even get an interest payment on the remaining money left in the contract, plus considerable, but legal, deductions on his personal income tax. No sooner had I presented the proposed

112 } Foster contract to the Doubleday clan than I got a phone call in my hotel room from John O'Donnell, the number one financial guy at Doubleday. He suggested I introduce the deferred compensation idea to help finalize the Foster contract.

The way it would work, if Foster would leave the $1 million signing bonus in deferred comp and learn to live on his $1 million-plus a year, the Mets would, after a couple of years, grant him a lifetime income of $300,000 a year, plus other financial perks. It all sounded dazzling to me. I'm sure it was the first time such an offer was made in baseball. One other mind-boggling fact: The prime lending rate at that time was 14.5 percent. That's right, 14.5 percent!

I met Foster's agent the next morning and explained our latest offer, which also included the cleaning up of the outstanding details. He said he would have to consult with his principal and we agreed to meet the following morning. That next day he told me Foster was not interested in any deferred compensation, and that they had, he informed me in a positive tone, better plans for the signing bonus. We completed the negotiations shortly thereafter, leaving only the need to transfer the matter to an official written contract and produce the $1 million signing bonus check. With this accomplished, we had George Foster and his wife come to New York for the introductory press conference, which drew a large gathering. In his initial remarks, Foster predicted that nearby LaGuardia Airport would have to change its flight patterns when his potential home runs were filling the sky. I'm sure George said it with tongue in cheek, but it made glaring headlines in the tabloids the next day and was widely discussed on TV. And it is typical of what I call "the doctrine of the overpromise." That is a doctrine that I have always personally avoided. The reasons are obvious.

Foster's performance on the field was all right but certainly not spectacular. It was not what we expected. Within the next couple of years he was back in the front office seeking a change in his salary schedule. His $1 million signing bonus was all gone, he reluctantly confessed, and his yearly paycheck was under siege from other sources. When asked about the deferred compensation plan he was offered on his initial contract, Foster maintained it was news to him. His agent, he said, had never discussed that offer with him. Foster's finances seemed to be in shambles and it didn't appear to be his fault. He had entrusted those finances to his agent and the agent's band of supporters. I have always felt that George Foster would have been justified in using his big bat on something other than baseballs.

{ 113

In another rebuilding effort, we had signed Dave Kingman, a big hitter from the past who had been with the Mets in the mid-1970s. He provoked a few tabloid headlines when he came and a few more when he left. But he also hit 37 home runs in 1982, tying a club record, and had an impressive lifetime 442 homers. However, Kingman also had a dubious distinction of being a leader in strikeouts.

Tom Seaver, born George Thomas Seaver, was sometimes known as "Tom Terrific," "The Franchise," or "The Pitcher." These latter names were all well-deserved kudos for the best player ever to put on a Mets uniform. Anytime you talk about the New York Mets, you have to talk about Seaver. A future Hall of Famer, Seaver compiled an amazing record with the Mets. This included four seasons as a twenty-game winner, pitching five one-hit games and posting a 25-7 record in the world championship season of 1969. Over his twenty-year career, Tom racked up 311 wins and 3,640 strikeouts. In 1992 he received the highest percentage, 98.84, of Hall of Fame votes in history.

Long before I got to Gotham, the worst event in the Seaver story had already occurred. At the trade deadline in 1977, the people who were running the Mets at that time, in a move I could never understand or attempt to explain, traded Seaver to Cincinnati for a parcel of young players of no particular note. It was difficult to figure out who was the most incensed: Seaver himself or his legion of fans. He was gone but never forgotten. Each year the story was recycled as Seaver continued to pitch effectively for the Reds for the next five seasons.

In 1983 I had a chance to bring Seaver, then age thirty-nine, back to New York and, of course, I jumped at the opportunity. He struggled, as indicated by his 9-14 record, but it was good to have No. 41 back in the fold. At the end of that season, there was a compensation draft and we were able to protect only ten of our players. After much discussion and to protect the good young talent we had amassed in our rebuilding program, the decision was made not to put Seaver on the protection list. Since that final decision was up to me, I freely admit I made the decision not to protect "Tom Terrific." He was claimed by the Chicago White Sox, who had lost a player in the draft.

Part of the decision to leave Seaver exposed was the miscalculation that other clubs would not touch him because he belonged to New York, figuratively as well as literally, just like Brooks Robinson belonged in Baltimore, Carl Yastrzemski belonged in Boston, and so on. I was wrong. No such sentiment existed in baseball and Seaver was picked up by the White Sox, where he had two winning seasons before his numbers began to decline. I suppose I could say, in the words of that great song, "I took the blows and did it my way." I liked Tom Seaver personally. Everybody I knew liked him as a compelling player in a physical game. The best description I heard was "he was the quintessential professional." And he was protective about his personal life, his wife, Nancy, and his two daughters. I respected him for that.

When Seaver's career was over and we were having a one-on-one conversation about the future, I asked him whether he was interested in broadcasting, or had any interest in coaching and eventually managing. I remember him saying that he never expected to get the same personal satisfaction he got from pitching. He told me, "It's a sunny Sunday afternoon and the ballpark is packed, and you go out in the first inning and stand on the mound and look around and realize you are in charge. A great deal of what is going to happen depends on me. But that's in the past." Seaver had the courage of his convictions. He went back to California, bought property, planted grapes, and wanted to make wine. Not any kind of wine, but good wine. He wanted to produce good wine. You wouldn't have expected any less from "Tom Terrific."

19

Competing in the Apple

George Bamberger's tenure as manager didn't last long. It was easy to see that he never really adapted to returning to New York, where he had grown up in the borough of Staten Island. This was something I should have known. Not everybody can handle New York and the different pressures it presents. It can happen to managers, players, or even play-by-play announcers. Yes, and maybe executives, too. Among them was Bamberger, who after a career away from New York was managing unhappily in the Big Apple.

Not me. I loved working in New York, loved the pressure, and loved competing against George Steinbrenner and his Yankees.

As a matter of fact, I never was a great fan of George Steinbrenner, the late boss of the Yankees. I had a lot of great memories of the Yankees, going back to my school days in Baltimore, before that city had Major League status. We read daily of DiMaggio, Yogi, Mantle, and the rest. Mike Burke, who ran the club when they were owned by CBS, was a special friend and cohort of mine. Steinbrenner and his band of limited partners were a different breed. Competing with the other New York club through my tenure in the Big Apple, I was convinced that George really didn't love the game. Rather, as a supreme egotist, he loved only his own team. Most of all, he loved throwing his baseball wealth in your face.

From the very start, Steinbrenner showed a lot of interest in sports, maybe even more than in the family maritime shipping business where he acquired his initial fortune. After graduating from Williams College in western Massachusetts, where he was on the track team, Steinbrenner dabbled in football and basketball coaching at both the high school and college levels. Later, when he was running the family shipping company in Cleveland, he operated the Cleveland Pipers pro-basketball team. He first tried baseball with an unsuccessful attempt to purchase the Cleveland Indians.

When the opportunity presented itself, he gathered a host of limited partners and became the owner of the New York Yankees, where his thirty-seven-year tenure is reported to have left him, upon his death in 2010, with a billion-dollar estate and the most valuable franchise in professional sports. There is great debate within baseball as to what would have been Steinbrenner's fate if he had made the deal for the Cleveland ball club.

Early in the 1980s, I had mentioned to a local newspaper reporter that Yankee Stadium was located up in the Bronx "near the state penitentiary." Steinbrenner protested to the baseball commissioner, and the more he complained, the more ink the Mets got. In those early years, George questioned a lot of Met moves. But when those moves proved to be successful, he was quick to follow suit.

{ 117

For example, when the Mets announced that they were switching night game times from 8 p.m. to 7:30 p.m., George countered that eight o'clock was the starting hour for baseball in New York and the Yankees would always begin their games at eight. When the Mets began to outdraw the Yanks, virtually on a daily basis, the Bronx Bombers suddenly switched from 8 to 7:30. Soon, the Yanks were mirroring the Mets in a lot of little ways. All of this seemed to show that George was not the Big Boss in New York, as he seemed to think of himself. Steinbrenner loved to see the Yanks headlined on the back page of the New York tabloids. And he was disgruntled when New York's other team suddenly got more exposure than his club. He was even known to call his manager and coaches to complain.

With more money to gamble than any other franchise in the Majors, George was constantly driving up the cost of doing business.

As earlier described, in the early '80s, the Mets had drafted high school pitcher Dwight Gooden out of Tampa. Within two years, he was pitching in the Majors and setting all kinds of strikeout records. For these feats, he also garnered much media coverage, including the visible back page of the tabloids. Fully aware of the Gooden success, Steinbrenner went looking for an equal.

The Yankee scouting system soon identified an African American high school left-handed pitcher who lived in a trailer in North Carolina and had impressed scouts with his 98 mph fastball. To cut to the chase, the Yankees signed the youngster, Brien Taylor, in the first round, when their chance came up. He was a legitimate first-rounder, I guess, but an average first-rounder, who would typically draw about a $350,000 signing bonus. In one of their patented moves to gain publicity, the Yankees—I'm sure at George's direction, even though he was suspended from the game at that time—paid the untried pitcher a $1.5 million signing bonus. That was the most money any baseball club had ever given a high schooler.

As it turned out, Brien was only the second amateur player to be picked first overall in the draft never to reach the Major Leagues. Taylor pitched in the lower Minors for a couple of seasons then hurt his shoulder in an off-season barroom fistfight. His baseball career was effectively finished. If that was all there was to the Taylor story, it would have been just another of Steinbrenner's financial follies. But it was more than that. By raising the bar on what a club would pay for a high school youngster when he gave Taylor $1.5 million, it affected every other club in baseball. From that point on, the top kids coming out of high schools, still barely tested, were looking for million-dollar payouts. And their "advisers" (also known as agents) were urging them on.

Back at the Mets, we all tackled the '83 season with renewed vigor, but early in June, Bamberger decided he couldn't take it anymore and resigned, leaving veteran coach Frank Howard to take charge as interim manager the rest of the way. In spite of all outward negatives—the loss of Seaver, four losing seasons since I became GM, and the manager quitting in midseason—I felt we were close to turning this team around in 1984. I had promised Nelson Doubleday it would take four or five years to rebuild the organization. Even giving me a pass on 1980 since I didn't join the club till spring training and had absolutely nothing to do with its formation, I now had spent the last three years on the job, and the natives had taken note.

When we were in spring training in St. Petersburg, Florida, Phil Pepe, a columnist at the *New York Daily News*, stunned me when he inquired, "Frank, you promised to make this club a contender in four or five years. Well, it's 1984 and the fifth year is coming up. If you don't get it done this year, would you consider retiring?" I knew the clock was ticking but I never considered retiring. Just then I began to imagine what the press was going to do to me if there was another bad year.

I knew Pepe from my time in the sports writing business, and he was a first-class journalist. His question was tough but fair. After a few seconds of reflection, I told him that, yes, I would consider walking away, but I was confident the job was done and that 1984 was going to be a turnaround year. The first step a GM has to take in rebuilding is to get his club to .500. Next, people will quiz you as to why .500 is important. You aren't going to win a pennant playing .500 baseball, they warn.

I've always considered .500 a significant benchmark because baseball is such a numerically oriented game. Once you get to .500, you are bordering on respectability. If you can win eleven out of every twenty games, that's .550 baseball. That translates to eighty-nine or ninety wins for the season. Anytime you can post those figures, you are in the pennant race. The Mets had sixty-eight wins and ninety-four losses in the 1983 season. So the next step, I believed, was to get to .500 baseball, winning as many as we lost over the whole season.

Building a Winner

By October of 1983, our search for a new manager was under way. I had in mind three candidates for the job. One was a former MLB manager; another, a longtime Major League coach, and Davey Johnson, who had not yet managed in the Majors. When it came down to the interviews, I felt our best chance would be with Davey Johnson. Davey had worked for me successfully as a Minor League manager the past two seasons and had been a good Major League ballplayer for the Orioles and the Atlanta Braves. Having given Johnson his first managing job in organized Minor League baseball and ultimately his first in the big leagues, I have a special sweet spot in my memory for my old Orioles second baseman. Johnson played with the O's from 1965 to 1972 and was the starting second baseman during the years the O's won four American League pennants. From the O's he went on to play for the Braves, Phillies, and Cubs and spent some time in the Japanese league. Davey was a bright, bright young man who had completed his BA degree in mathematics at Trinity University in San Antonio during the winter terms while playing professional baseball the rest of the year.

I remember one of Davey's first attempts to use his mathematical education in baseball. While playing for the Orioles, he was convinced that he should be batting further up in the lineup than manager Earl Weaver decreed. Using an early version of a computer, he worked out a whole series of complex lineups that proposed to show that it would be a vastly more efficient club with Johnson batting in a higher, key spot in the batting order. Rumor about Johnson's pending scheme had spread among the clubhouse fraternity, so several days later, when he went into Weaver's office with an armload of paper, the troops were silently waiting and watching.

The O's manager was busy with paperwork, but he stopped and looked puzzled as he turned his attention to Johnson. Davey began to explain his visit and Weaver seemed to get more aggravated as his second baseman droned on. When the visitor began to reach for the first page of his exhibit, Weaver reached out and calmly guided the whole stack of paper off his desk and into the neighboring trash can. With that, he stood up, and in a less than patient voice, said a few harsh words and sternly indicated that the meeting was over. What had Weaver said? Later, I learned that it was "No goddamn machine is going to tell me how to write my lineup. I damn well will do it my way, and you can take all of your damn theories back to college." { 121

As the Mets' new manager, Johnson brought with him a fire-balling, nineteen-year-old pitcher named Dwight Gooden, whom he had managed at Lynchburg, Virginia, a Single-A club, the year before. I had not wanted to take Gooden to the Majors so quickly, but Johnson persuaded me to think otherwise. Davey was right. That first year, Gooden posted a 17-9 record with 276 strikeouts and a 2.60 ERA. It was the start of a great Major League career for the youngster out of Tampa, better known in baseball as "Doc" Gooden. I never knew where the name "Doc" came from, but it sure seemed to fit when he operated on the mound with surgical skill. After that 17-9 season in 1984, Dwight was the toast of baseball and continued to be a winning pitcher for years to come despite his widely publicized personal problems.

Sensing that big years lay ahead after two significant additions—Keith Hernandez and Gary Carter—and moving Strawberry up from the Minors, I felt Davey Johnson was the right manager to take us to the next step. The rebuilding process was all but over by that time. In what I have described as "the turnaround year," the New Yorkers went 90-72 in 1984 and finished second behind the Chicago Cubs. Remember, the previous year, 1983, the Mets were 68-94.

With Davey Johnson taking command of the field forces, things started to drop into place elsewhere, helping the cause from the bottom up. By that I mean the farm system was functioning from the rookie leagues to Triple-A, and we were spitting out Major League ballplayers—Major League, winning ballplayers.

Darryl Strawberry, Wally Backman, Jose Oquendo, and, of course, Keith Hernandez were all on that '84 spring training roster, plus some pitching help. When Bamberger was in his second season, things were not going too well and he pleaded with me to bring the twenty-one-year-old Strawberry up to the big league club. Straw, whom I had drafted in 1980, was shining at Triple-

122 }   A Norfolk and I was convinced he should stay right there. But knowing Bambi's disposition, I put aside my feelings about proper development and brought the slugging left-handed hitter to New York in May of 1983. Right from the start, Strawberry began to carve out a successful Major League career. But I continue to feel that if I had held him longer at Norfolk, he would have been even bigger in the big leagues.

The New York press had stamped me as being too cautious in handling fledgling stars. I guess I would have to plead guilty to that charge. But even before baseball, I had learned that patience is an important virtue, and I submit that such thinking is a virtual necessity in baseball.

Our trade for the Cardinals' Keith Hernandez, a defensive genius and a good left-handed hitter, actually fell into our laps. It happened like this. I got a call from Joe McDonald, ironically the ex–general manager of the Mets, whom I had released from that post when I took over the club. Joe seemed to understand the move, and we remained friends as he went to St. Louis and worked with his buddy Whitey Herzog, the Cardinals' skipper.

"Have you ever thought about trading Neil Allen?" McDonald asked. The inquiry startled me and I quickly blurted out, "No, I never have. He's an important part of our relief pitching staff and seems to be getting better every year." Actually, Allen had had fifty-nine saves over the past three seasons. "Well," said Joe, "if you will talk about Allen, we'll talk about Keith Hernandez." If I was startled with his question, I was absolutely stunned when he mentioned Hernandez. There was a player I had admired from afar but never dreamed would become available.

My answer was brief and to the point: "Let's talk," and talk we did, for about an hour, and then agreed to resume the next morning, which we did. By afternoon we had completed the deal. McDonald had insisted he should get something besides Allen for Hernandez and I couldn't disagree with him over that. So the bulk of the talk was about what that "extra" would be. You don't want to overpay, but at the same time you don't want to blow the deal. {123}

Opportunities like this one didn't come up too often, and I reacted accordingly. Having ownership's confidence and the right to make significant changes in a club without lengthy owner input is the secret to getting these kinds of maneuvers completed. I knew that in adding Hernandez I had considerably improved our ball club as I began to jot down a possible lineup. Did Keith bat third, or fourth, or even fifth? But while the exercise was fun, it brought the realization that I wasn't going to make that decision; it was going to be made by manager Davey Johnson.

As happy as we were to get Keith Hernandez, he did not come to New York without some "warts." To begin with, he couldn't understand why he was traded by the Cardinals. He had been drafted by St. Louis and had played his whole career with the Redbirds. He was brutally frank and informed me when we first talked that he was unhappy about being traded to New York. He didn't like New York and its National League ball club and he intended to get out of town as soon as possible. Rather than pick a fight with him over his apparent unhappiness, I quietly told him he had to give New York a chance, that it actually was a great place to be a ballplayer. I added that the rest of our staff was ready to assist him in the transition.

Under Davey Johnson's guidance, Keith responded well to playing in the Big Apple. In fact, he soon was one of the club's leaders. I watched carefully as, in a year or two, he became the quintessential New Yorker. So much for that wart!

21

Breaking .500

As promised, things turned around in 1984. We flew by the .500 stop
and went on to vault into the pennant race as Johnson steered the
club to our 90-72 record, a virtual reversal of the previous year's
dismal mark. If I had to pick, I'd say that Gooden and Hernandez
were the chief contributors to the achievement, but maybe that
is unfair, because there were several other standouts. Gooden,
who was then nineteen years of age, had but a single full season
in the Minors and posted his 17-9 Major League mark. Hernandez,
very much living up to expectations, hit .311 for the season and
drove in ninety-four runs.

The club finished second in the Eastern Division race and
drew a million more in attendance than it had in 1979, the year
before Doubleday became involved. Others instrumental in the
turnaround were an ever-improving Darryl Strawberry, who hit
twenty-six home runs and had ninety-six RBIs; Rusty Staub, who
had eleven pinch hits, all of which seemed to come at crucial points
in the proceedings; and Jesse Orosco, a stylish left-handed relief
pitcher who had been traded from Cleveland and who began his
career with the Mets with thirty-one saves.

By adding Hernandez, we now had a good ball club, a competitive ball club. But was it good enough to win a National League
pennant or World Series? All signs pointed to that, but my gut
told me we could use another big hitter, a real home run hitter.
That was easier said than done.

Searching the Major League rosters and taking all the advice

I could get from our baseball staff, there were no apparent candidates. That meant we were going to have to entice a big league franchise into a deal if we were going to get a big slugger. And what were we going to use for bait? We wrote down all the players we considered untouchables, and held our breath on the rest.

After several false starts, I called my friend John McHale, the GM of the Montreal Expos, and took my time getting to the real purpose of the call. First, I asked him what he was looking for to improve his ball club. He mentioned a third baseman. I then got around to asking him about Gary Carter, his All-Star, power-hitting catcher. As I remember, McHale's quick response to my question was that if it ever became public that he was talking about trading Carter, he would be run out of Canada. Well, I responded, we have a young third baseman, an outstanding prospect, that I could place in a trade for Carter. We at least ought to continue to talk. He halfheartedly agreed, and I promised that nobody needed to know what we were discussing and the secret was secure as far as the Mets were concerned.

The young third baseman I was talking about was Hubie Brooks, whom we had already listed among the untouchables. But for a ballplayer the caliber of Carter, I was ready, willing, and able to yank Brooks off any list. Approximately two months later, after some ten phone calls and two face-to-face meetings, McHale and I had a deal. The basic part of that deal was that Carter was traded to New York and Brooks to Montreal.

On our side of the table, the only other person to know of the pending deal was my number one guy, Al Harazin. Near the end, I had told my owners that something big was brewing, but they never asked for the particulars. My owners were very special people.

While the success of the 1984 season had caught the New York fans by surprise, it was welcome but not surprising to me. The major thought from the New York press was a basic question: Can the Mets keep up the pace they achieved the past season, or will they fall back to the losing habits of the old Mets?

I thought the addition of Carter, coming on the heels of the Hernandez acquisition, was a giant step. I have always considered Carter to be the final link in the rebuilding chain. He spent little time adapting to his new team. He contributed to that good '85 club right away, hitting thirty-four home runs and, as a veteran catcher, complementing a young pitching staff.

One of those young pitchers was a right-handed relief pitcher from our ever-improving farm system, Roger McDowell. Early on, McDowell had bone chips removed from his elbow by our orthopedic specialist, Jim Parkes. Post-operation, McDowell's fastball had a lot of "sink" and was very effective. Teamed with Jesse Orosco, the duo gave us a first-class pair out of the bullpen, one a right-hander, the other a lefty. The starting pitching staff we had put together with the assistance of Al Harazin and Joe McIlvaine, our director of scouting, was composed of the aforementioned Ron Darling and Doc Gooden, Bobby Ojeda, acquired from the Boston Red Sox, and { 127 Sid Fernandez, a Los Angeles product for whom we had also traded.

Thus, out of our own system we had a starter, but the three others came via trades. That is the way to build a winning ball club. Of course, in the previous two years, we had also traded for Keith Hernandez and Gary Carter.

I was often criticized for trades that I made—and I made a lot of them, some good, some not so good. But I'm a great believer in such transactions. Show me a general manager who hasn't made a trade and I'll show you a GM who will not succeed. I once had a general manager scold me, saying, "Why are you trying to make trades? If you don't, they can't get mad at you."

Trades were especially attractive to me at the annual baseball winter meetings. "I'll do this and you do that" was the basic approach to fellow GMs. Today, it's much more complicated, with both owners and players' agents involved. My trading practice was simple. When I saw a player I liked, I'd write down his name. When his name came up, even years later, I would try to figure a way to land him for our team.

Just getting good players is not enough. The team chemistry has to be right. I've seen players of equal abilities on the same club who are winners and others who are losers. This may sound a bit arrogant, but during my days with the Orioles, my axiom for making trades or bringing up Minor Leaguers was simple: "Is he an Orioles ballplayer?" We expected them to be the best year after year, and for a string of years, they were the best.

The following year, 1985, was another promising one as the Mets finished with a 98-64 record, but trailed St. Louis by three games in the Eastern Division. It was evident that a league championship was getting closer. In the final weeks of the '85 season, the Mets made a run at the Eastern Division–leading Cardinals. I well remember being in St. Louis for the series that would go a long way toward deciding the Eastern Division race.

Our hotel was downtown, with Busch Stadium nearby. Also downtown, on the banks of the Mississippi River, was the ancient Roman Catholic cathedral that by this time was a parish church. And since activities at the ballpark didn't commence until 5 p.m., it was not unusual for me to visit the church for the midday Mass. I had been at the church two or three days in a row and noted that following the regular Mass, the Monsignor would urge parishioners to join him in special prayers for the daily success of the St. Louis Cardinals baseball team.

One day, I greeted the Monsignor after the Mass and in a half-jovial manner told him that there were other individuals in the church who favored the New York Mets over the Cardinals. He smiled broadly, took my arm, and in a pontifical voice informed me, "Son, you need to remember that the Cardinals are the parish team."

So the Mets, after challenging at the highest levels in both 1984 and 1985, appeared to be ready to win it all. That was my assessment, and manager Davey Johnson felt the same way as we headed into spring training in 1986.

Dominating Season

As the 1986 season approached, we felt the team was ready to make a run at the big prize. In spring training Davey Johnson told his players he expected to win it all. Not only that, he said he expected to dominate. Johnson's orders in Florida in 1986 proved prophetic. The Mets dominated the Eastern Division of the National League, then the NL playoffs, and went on to that historic win over the Boston Red Sox in the World Series. { 129

It was the end of a six-year journey for me. The fulfillment of a promise I made to Nelson Doubleday when he hired me to run his club in 1980—the world championship!

In my mind, four players stood out throughout the regular 162-game season. Veterans Keith Hernandez and Gary Carter were rock solid all the way. Not surprisingly, so were two younger players—outfielder Darryl Strawberry and pitcher Dwight Gooden.

Carter drove in 105 runs to lead the club in that department and Hernandez hit .310 while earning his ninth straight Gold Glove at first base. Strawberry hit 27 homers and had 93 RBIS while Gooden posted a 17-6 record, striking out over 200 hitters for a second straight year.

There were other luminaries that season, especially pitchers. Lefty Bob Ojeda won eighteen games while losing five and lived up to all the promise I foresaw when I first laid eyes on him at a Minor League game in Pawtucket, Rhode Island. Ron Darling was 15-6 and compiled a 2.81 ERA. Young Sid Fernandez, the Hawaii native, won sixteen and lost six, and a couple of bullpen specialists—Jesse Orosco and Roger McDowell—worked their trade in a special way. The right-hander, McDowell, made twenty-five appearances with twenty-two saves, and Orosco, the left-hander, had twenty-one saves.

The club won 108 games that '86 season, the finest performance ever by a Mets club. They took over first place in the Eastern Division on April 23 and never looked back. In early September, the Mets were twenty-two games ahead of second-place Philadelphia and had already clinched the division title. That, of course, brought on the perennial discussion about whether it is advantageous to win your division title early so your club is well rested for the playoffs, or to win it late so regular-season sharpness carries into the postseason games. That was the case in 2011 when the St. Louis Cardinals improbably made it to the playoffs as the wild card on the last day of the season, then went on to win the World Series. As somebody whose club has won it both early and late, I'll take the former.

The New York press described the '86 Mets as a cocky bunch playing with a swagger. As someone who had seen it before in some of our good Orioles teams, I prefer to say that the Mets performed with a noticeable degree of confidence. They had fun playing and they were fun to watch. Every couple of weeks, it seemed, they were breaking some old Mets mark, and those new records seemed to come with consummate ease. Young ballplayers with talent and ability are not much different from the successful Wall Street types. The '86 Mets came from a background of achievement—in little league, high school, college, and Minor Leagues. They were a stripe above most and they reflected it in the MLB. They were not showing off; they were confident young men.

We were the toast of the town, and the observant and oft-critical New York press was singing our praises. It was not always so. As a former sportswriter, I understood and appreciated the important job of the press. But being the general manager and spokesman for the Orioles and the Mets quickly taught me that the view is different from the other side. Maybe I'm thin-skinned, but I found it unacceptable for a baseball writer, maybe a year or two out of college, to set himself up as a the chief critic of a veteran manager or general manager. To be frequently misquoted does not go down well either, especially if it's deliberate. One time I confronted a reporter who had quoted me without ever having interviewed me. His response: "I wrote what I thought you would have said if I had interviewed you." In New York the media focus was intense. Everything was magnified. Of course, it was not just the print media. Every time I'd walk on the field at Shea Stadium TV crews were ready to stick a microphone in my face. You had to be ready to respond on the spot and accurately. The toughest job is to be consistent. You had to remember what you had said previously to another reporter. All in all, I can't think of any better way to become a general manager than being a writer and learning the game from the standpoint of one who reports it.

The next step was the National League playoffs. Western Division winner Houston would play the Mets in a best-of-seven series that proved to be a classic series throughout. The Houston Astros had a formidable pitching staff, headed by Mike Scott, a former Met who seemed to always be at his very best when he pitched against his old team. We were virtually certain that Scott's best pitch was a cut fastball, an illegal pitch, because we believed the surface of the ball was cut with a metal object—like a belt buckle—before it was thrown. The result was a pitch that causes the thrown ball to make strange moves as it approaches the plate. The "cut" fastball is not to be confused with today's "cutter," which describes the way a ball is thrown and is perfectly legal. A discussion with baseball officials prior to the start of the series proved useless. They ignored our objections and claimed that if there was any illegal maneuver, it would be handled by the umpires. I suppose they felt that any such claims, if made public, would detract from one of the game's proudest moments.

Scott beat Gooden, 1–0, in the opening game at the Houston Astrodome, and one had to surmise that whatever Scott threw, he threw it well. He was a darned good pitcher and a great competitor. Why did the Mets ever let him go? New York won the next game, 5–1, behind Bobby Ojeda's pitching. Then it was back to Shea Stadium where Lenny Dykstra's two-run homer pulled Game Three out of the fire, 6–5.

That "Met Killer," Mr. Scott, was due to pitch on Sunday. Playing on our home field, we had control over the balls so were in a position to investigate the "suspected doctored" balls we thought he was throwing. So, after the umps ostensibly checked the new baseballs in the dressing room, they were turned over to the home club for distribution over the course of the game. And when they were thrown out of the game by the umpires, the balls went back to the bench from whence they had come.

After discussing the matter with Davey Johnson, we instructed the ball boys that every ball tossed out of the game when Scott was pitching was to be placed in a special bag and not mixed with the other removed balls. A postgame inspection of the special bag of baseballs showed a preponderance of the balls had been cut after Scott got hold of them on the mound. Apparently they were rendered illegal by a belt buckle, a ring, something inside a glove, or tampered with in any number of ways. The baseball elite still seemed unimpressed, asking how they could be positive that we weren't scarring the balls after they left the playing field just to prove our case. While we struck out off the field with our protest, we also lost on the field. Mike Scott evened up the series at two all that Sunday with a three-hit, one-run performance in a 3–1 Astros victory.

After a day off there came another classic game. Gooden and that all-time all-star Nolan Ryan hooked up in a memorable pitching duel that saw the New York team prevail, 2–1, when Gary Carter singled home the winning run in the twelfth inning. But this time the ending belonged to the bullpen. Now it was back to Houston for the finishing contests with the Mets needing just one more win to get to the World Series. Rumors abounded that

Scott would be back for the seventh game if only Houston could get a win in the pending sixth.

Game Six was a classic of all classics. The Mets needed a victory to clinch it and Houston hoped for a win to set up Mike Scott to pitch in a seventh-game finale. There was a flurry of hype for the game, and the contest lived up to every bit of it. This was the toughest game—and longest—I ever had to sit through. The game went sixteen innings, and when it ended at four hours and forty-three minutes, it set a record for the longest playoff game ever.

Houston scored three runs in the first inning and it stayed that way until the top of the ninth when Mookie Wilson, Keith Hernandez, and Ray Knight all singled home a run to send the game into extra innings. In the fourteenth inning, the Mets got a single run, but the Astros answered with a homer in the bottom half and the game went on. In the top of the sixteenth inning, Strawberry doubled and Knight singled to spark a three-run rally { 133 and it looked like the Mets had it won. But Houston came back in the bottom of the inning with two runs and had the winning runners on base when Jesse Orosco struck out the final batter. Orosco, basically a short reliever, had three of the four wins in the series. So we finally prevailed in six games.

Back in New York, TV sets and radios were tuned to the afternoon game in record numbers. Office workers were still hanging around, refusing to leave work while the game was still in question. On the commuter lines, heading out of the city, conductors were doing play-by-play for an attentive and appreciative audience of homeward-bound riders. Forgotten in the moment of exhilaration was the looming ultimate test in the World Series—against the Boston Red Sox, a team determined to break the sixty-eight-year Curse of the Bambino.

23

Infamous Plane Trip

In Houston our celebration was just beginning, which led to an infamous plane ride back to New York. There have been more than a few versions published about what took place that night on the return from the playoff win in Houston. In an effort to set the record straight, it's worth going back to the beginning, which includes my previous experience in Baltimore. With the Orioles, when we got to a World Series, we invited the wives of both players and coaches and other traveling personnel to travel on the team plane. We also provided hotel accommodations for this season-ending series. I think every Major League club that qualified for the world championship in those days provided the same plum. Baltimore was not alone in the practice.

All that changed in 1969, when playoffs prior to the World Series became part of season-ending baseball. This presented another set of questions. My decision then was, and still would be, to leave wives and others at home. Concentrate on prevailing in those playoffs and after that, extend travel accommodations to spouses. This latter practice alone caused enough problems. Could unmarried players invite their "significant others"? If the wife found it impossible to leave a child home, could she bring along a son or a daughter? A mother or a father? In-laws? The answer to these questions was "no," and I often felt we had as many upset with us about that as the O's had success with extending travel invites only for the World Series. I had announced that the same regulations would prevail for the Mets.

Having won the NL East by mid-September, team personnel had a lot of time (perhaps too much) to think about the pending playoffs. Two weeks later, my secretary, Jean Coen, who also was my administrative assistant (and a good one), told me that a couple of ballplayers had called the office and wanted to set up an appointment. "Who and why?" was my reply. Jean, in her usual patient manner, said Ron Darling and Ray Knight and that she didn't know the specific reason for their request. She had already set up the date and the time, and feeling she had the situation in hand, I promptly forgot about the matter.

A couple days later—or it might have been the very next day—Jean warned me that Darling and Knight were arriving for a morning appointment, so I wasn't surprised when they were shown into the office. After some small talk about how much they had enjoyed the season and were looking forward to the playoffs, they got around to the purpose of their visit. The whole squad, they claimed, would like the Mets to rescind their previous announcement and allow the players to take the wives to Houston for those road games. I'll give them this: They were well prepared, and one could quickly fathom some feminine influence in their preparation. They responded to my argument about my experience in Baltimore by replying that this wasn't Baltimore, it was New York, and things were done differently in the Big Apple.

Apparently, knowing of my deep interest in attendance, they pointed out that the Mets had set attendance marks the past two seasons and that the club must have had positive financial results. My firm retort was it was not about cost. I pointed out that the club had not yet won anything but the division and there remained a couple of giant steps before we won the big battle—the World Series. They then dragged out the old argument that the wives were a calming influence on the road—a premise to which I don't necessarily subscribe. It was a discussion rather than an argument and concluded quietly. I was impressed with the quality of the players' messengers and told them I would

{ 135

give the matter some additional thought and get back to them in a couple of days.

Was I short-sighted? This was the question I asked myself. Looking at the team's record on the road, one would have to conclude that it did a great job playing away from New York. I couldn't see how it could be improved by adding wives. My mind was settled on the question, but I did ask for opinions from the manager and some of his coaches and other staff people, including several females. The reviews were mixed. One thing became certain: the final decision was up to me. With more opinions than I needed, I personally still felt it was a bad idea but, not having the courage of my own convictions, agreed to invite the wives of the uniformed players on the final trip to Houston.

All of this added up to Game Six and that final nail-biting sixteen-inning battle. There were no surprises in what followed. The champagne bottles were popped open in record time in the Astros' visiting clubhouse and the idiotic tradition of squirting each other with the bubbly commenced. Occasionally, somebody took a few swigs from the bottle. More than a few traded the champagne for beer and the atmosphere gradually switched from squirting to drinking, which went on and on. About that time somebody thought of the ladies. One or more of the adventuresome females sent word that the lounge to which they had been assigned had some thirsty citizens. Additional festivities soon started up there.

A chartered plane was lined up to get the club back to New York. This was not the first such experience for the plane crew, and a ready bar and first-class food awaited. The biggest task then was to get the revelers out of the Houston Astrodome, on to the chartered buses, and eventually to the plane. I had four or five years of experience in a similar drill and it's never easy. It's unbelievable how some people can get lost between the stadium and the chartered plane. A happy breath is drawn when the whole gang is present and accounted for. Believe me, I'm no party pooper. I'll drink my share during the clubhouse celebration, but I refuse to pour perfectly drinkable drinks on some of my fellow celebrants. Besides, there are live TV cameras all over the clubhouse waiting to catch revelers in an unguarded moment. Once on the plane and with a couple more rounds of drinks under the belt, the food, and plenty of it, was brought out. Then one of the women, who apparently had been "overserved," picked up a dinner roll and hurled it at someone across the aisle. That started it. Soon there was a huge food fight under way as others joined the fray.

I was sitting in the front of the plane and can't vouch for everything that happened farther back. Were some of the players involved? I've heard yes and no from some who had better views than I. But it went on for some time until cooler heads, including mine when I went back, prevailed. I then went forward to my seat and finally got to eat dinner.

The middle of the plane was littered as a result of the food battle, and some seats were broken. The damage was $7,000-plus and the airline rightly billed us. After initially trying to have the players pay for the damage, the manager thought otherwise and the Mets picked up the tab. After this time, I no longer blame the ladies for the damage, and I count myself responsible. I had agreed to invite the wives when I had the choice. I just didn't have the courage of my own convictions.

New York fans would soon be enjoying their first World Series since the Yankees met the Dodgers in 1981. The Mets' only two previous World Series appearances had been in 1973 and 1969.

Series Showdown

The "Amazin' Mets" were the creatures of another generation. That was back in 1969 when the New Yorkers won the World Series by upsetting the favored Baltimore Orioles, a team I headed and thought to be the best in baseball. Now suddenly that title was resuscitated to fit the 1986 team as it prepared to face the Boston Red Sox in the World Series.

That '69 season had a special spot in Met fan memories. In fact, when I first got to Shea Stadium in 1980 to take over, more than one of the veteran employees told me the goal should be to match the 1969 club. That, they said, was the key to bringing fans back to the stadium in Queens. But the glory year, I reasoned, had been two generations ago. It made better sense to concentrate on appealing to younger baseball fans to produce a new set of Mets admirers. And we had really succeeded in that quest during the dominating season of 1986.

For the first time, the 1980s would clearly be the decade of the Mets in terms of prominence, attendance, and the Big Apple's attention. After losing to the LA Dodgers in the 1981 World Series, the Yankees would go pennant-less for the remainder of the decade.

But, of course, the Yankees had been *the* team in town for most of the time since the Mets arrived as an expansion team in 1962. Going back further in Yankee lore, some of the most colorful stories involve two pinstripe legends—Casey Stengel and Yogi Berra. Long before there was a Mets team in New York, Stengel managed the Yankees. Nicknamed "The Old Professor," he was one of baseball's most colorful and quotable characters. Stengel is at the center of some of the game's most amusing stores—or maybe tall tales.

One story from his managerial years that I've always found entertaining was when Casey called a clubhouse meeting of the Yankees to discuss reports that team members were spending too much time socializing in bars and womanizing. Casey reportedly said, "Don't think you're fooling me about all the nightclubs and playing around. There's even a case of gonorrhea in the clubhouse." To which catcher Yogi Berra reportedly piped up, "Thank God, I'm getting tired of drinking this Yoo-hoo," referring to a chocolate drink of the time.

Both Stengel and Berra were often characterized as clowns, but both were very smart and wise observers of the game of baseball. In addition to his baseball life, Stengel, a great tactician, also was a licensed dentist, a fact few ever knew.   { 139

I remember attending the All-Star Game in St. Louis in 1966, the maiden year of the old Busch Stadium. The temperature was well over 100 degrees at game time. Stengel was asked what he thought of the new ballpark. He replied, "Well, it holds the heat very well." During his twelve-year reign (1949–60) as Yankee manager, Stengel's teams amassed seven World Series championships. He ended his career in 1962 as the first manager of the expansion New York Mets. Berra, too, had a managerial stint with the Mets in the early 1970s.

The impending 1986 showdown between the Mets and Red Sox was going to be special for me for another reason. My friend Lou Gorman, who was the rival Red Sox GM and an excellent baseball exec, had worked with me twice: first with the Orioles, before going to Kansas City, and then to Seattle as general manager of the Mariners. He then moved back to New York to help us rebuild the Mets.

Sometime in 1984 I received a call from the top executive in Boston, asking permission to talk with Lou. When I inquired as to what they had in mind, he told me they were interested in making Lou general manager of the Red Sox. Since Lou was born and raised in nearby Rhode Island and had been a lifelong Red Sox fan, I knew instantly they were talking about Lou's dream job. I quickly gave permission. Just as quickly, I called Lou into my office to tell him the good news. He confirmed my feelings about this as his dream job. We parted, and he and his lovely wife, Mary Lou, moved on to Beantown. In just three seasons, Lou had helped produce the best club in the American League in 1986, and Boston was starved for a World Series win, having waited since 1918 for a Series championship. The Series would open in New York for the first two of the seven-game competition. Then we moved to Boston for the next three and, as necessary, back to New York for the final two.

Things didn't start out that well for our side, and playing before the home crowd, we quickly found ourselves two down to Boston. Ron Darling pitched valiantly in the opener, scattering five hits and an unearned run over seven innings, and McDowell was perfect over the final two. Boston had scored their one run in the top of the seventh when second baseman Tim Teufel's error allowed Jim Rice to score. That was plenty for Boston ace Bruce Hurst, who shut us out with a four-hit performance over the first eight. Calvin Schiraldi, another former Mets farmhand, eased through the ninth in relief for a 1–0 Boston victory in Game One.

Gooden, the ace of the Mets' pitching staff, got bombed in Game Two. Things looked dark as the Red Sox prevailed again, 9–3.

We traveled to Boston for Games Three, Four, and Five, and things improved. It started with the first pitch. Lead-off batter Lenny Dykstra smacked one over the fence in Fenway Park to give us the lead. Behind the fine pitching of Ojeda and McDowell's two innings of relief, the Mets made it look easy. We had the win, 7–1, but were still down two games to one in the Series.

Ron Darling took care of that in the middle Boston game, holding the Red Sox to four hits and no runs over seven innings.

Although McDowell gave up two runs in relief, Orosco came on to put an end to the Sox scoring. Carter's bat accounted for two home runs and three of the six Mets runs as New York won, 6–2. Now with the Series tied at two apiece, Gooden drew the assignment in Game Five. But once again he failed and lost his second straight, 4–2, despite Sid Fernandez's four innings of shutout relief.

It was back to New York for Game Six with the Mets facing elimination and an end to their championship dreams. The rest is history—as I have already described. The Mets went on to win the next two games in unbelievable fashion and proudly owned the world title.

It seemed to me that the Mets had a lot of heroes in that World Series, and Ray Knight won the Most Valuable Player Award. The New York bullpen was great throughout. All four of our winning pitchers in the Series had come to us via trades as we were building that pennant contender. Knight, Carter, and Hernandez also came the same way.

One of the top prizes for winning the World Series, at least as far as the city of New York is concerned, is the ticker-tape parade. The 1986 world champion Mets were not denied that pleasure. The parade starts deep in the Wall Street area and, behind a police escort, wanders up to Midtown. Throughout, the sidewalks are packed and the players are bombed by a clutter of paper, ticker-tape particularly, coming from the upper floors of the financial houses along the way.

Not surprisingly, Nelson Doubleday excused himself from the festivities, and Fred Wilpon and family went off in the first car. Jean and I were assigned to the second convertible and a subsequent flood of good wishes ensued. Until we shoved off to start the parade, I had been busily counting the ballplayers and getting them to their proper vehicles. They seemed to be just as excited as the waiting crowds. The first couple of cars moved off without interruption, but there was a pause in the proceedings early on. Some traffic breakdown occurred, I recall, and the

{ 141

leading vehicles arrived at the planned destination long before the rest. New York governor Mario Cuomo waited patiently to preside over the official ceremonies.

Cuomo, as is well known, had played Minor League baseball in the Pittsburgh Pirates system, had been a scout and was still a major fan. I wanted to talk politics with him and he wanted to talk baseball, so we had an interesting and lively discussion until the lagging cars caught up and the ceremonies began. I don't remember much about the speeches that followed, including my own, but I vividly recall our discussions, some of which touched on whether the governor would run for president, which eventually he declined to do.

25

Futures Trading

The 1986 World Series celebration went on for a while, but I have always found that one is better off quickly closing down the past and working on the future. We learned a host of things, good and bad, from the Series, all valuable in addressing the task ahead. Almost immediately, the subject of contracts came up. Agents started calling as soon as I was back in my office. No doubt they felt it was advantageous to get to me while the euphoria of a world championship might soften me up.

It's a major mistake to begin contract talks in the post-Series bedlam. My feeling is that such talks should begin later in the winter when you have a better picture of where you are going.

A good example of this is the disappointing experience I had with Ray Knight. Ray was the Series MVP and a valuable contributor in the playoffs and, in fact, throughout the whole season. We had added him to cover as a veteran infielder, particularly at third base. His stock suddenly skyrocketed in those final weeks of the 1986 campaign. Up to that point I had given serious thought to trading Knight, who would soon turn thirty-five, or releasing him after the season concluded. I had made a decision some years before not to allow my team to get old together. (I shake my head in wonder, incidentally, when good teams repeatedly make what I consider the serious error of not following this principle.)

Knight, by the way, was married to Nancy Lopez, who, at that time, was among the top women's golfers in the world. And, as far as I was concerned, she was one of the nicest women, in and out of sports, in the world. When Nancy came to a ballgame, and she came to a lot of games, she asked to sit with the other wives—nothing special, no private box seats, no fuss, no bother.

As it happened, I offered Ray a one-year contract with a healthy raise—actually a reward for his 1986 season. Knight's agent, however, insisted it was going to take at least a two-year agreement for Ray to rejoin the Mets. Having watched Ray's efforts throughout the season and appreciating his performance, I still felt his best days were behind him and he was fast approaching the end of the trail. This time with the courage of my own convictions, I refused to give in on the length of the contract—one year. In these circumstances, you never get to talk to the player, only his agent. And that agent appeared to have convinced the Knights that he was deserving of a two-year pact.

I felt that if I could have talked to Ray privately and convinced him of my thinking, we would have come to an agreement. "Look, Ray," I would have said, "play next year; it's real good money, and at the end of that season, we'll talk again. Do you think you can play again or should we talk about going over to the administration? Do you want to coach, or start managing in the Minors? Or would you want a slot here in the office? Perhaps, by then you might have your sights set on scouting? Or, maybe, go into play-by-play on radio and TV? There are a lot of opportunities with the Mets."

Knight was a quality guy with good baseball instincts and we would have worked something out. But his agent said no dice. It was a two-year playing contract or goodbye. I reluctantly said goodbye. Every other team in baseball would have a crack at signing him. A couple of months later I heard that my old team, the Baltimore Orioles, had signed Knight to a two-year deal. When the contract was approved by the commissioner's office, we learned that the total pay for the two years was not as much as the Mets' one-year offer. Strange things happen. The next thing I heard was that the Knights had fired his agent. But Mr. Knight went on to

144 }

play Major League baseball for the next couple of years, although he never again reached the peak of that '86 season. After a managerial stint with the Cincinnati Reds, he got into broadcasting and today is part of the Washington Nationals broadcast team.

Always looking to the future, the next thing I did was to consult what I called my "wee-gee board." Whereas a Ouija board was meant to communicate with spirits, "wee-gee board" was my name for a system I used for a number of years and one that I considered to be successful each year. Here's how it worked. On my yellow legal pad, I kept a three-year future plan for my ball club. It was full of names in penciled-in boxes and full of my own personal faith and hope.

After the '86 World Series year, I remember that I had Wally Backman listed at second base for the coming year and the year after that. In the third year I had a question mark, in the event that I was unsure he could still be a classy second baseman three years out. But it was worth making that judgment a year beyond rather than at this time. If the original spot was still empty the following year, it meant we should be looking for a replacement. If we had a suitable candidate in the farm system, that was great. But if we didn't have one in the Minors, we were alerted to be looking for a trade that involved a second baseman. The scouts were notified when getting their assignments for the season that we, for instance, could be looking to trade for a second baseman and hence to be on the lookout for possible candidates. { 145

I kept track of other important topics on that yellow legal pad. One of these was important, even if unlikely: "What happens if the manager gets hit by a truck?"

Among the more likely to happen topics: my list of potential Major League managers. One column included young men who appeared to be ready to move into the big show. Another was a list of old Major League skippers whom I felt deserved another chance. There was another, shorter list of managers still plying their trade in the Major Leagues. If any were ever available in the future, they got my immediate attention. Slowly, word of my list got around and each year I had at least two calls from other GMS looking for information! On another page, I had a list of ballplayers who had impressed me when I looked at other clubs. I knew if they were offered in trade or, maybe, were free agents, I would be interested.

In earlier days, while I was still in Baltimore in the seventies and our club was playing on the West Coast, I had decided to go to New York and do a weekend of Mets viewing. I saw a couple of pitchers who would light up anybody, and there were three other ballplayers who struck my fancy. One was Mets first baseman Mike Jorgensen, who looked to be the best hitter on the club. Another was the shortstop who had already had some positive history. But my top choice was outfielder Ken Singleton, not just from what he showed that weekend but because his future was so full of promise. I was surprised when the Mets traded Singleton to Montreal, and when I later heard a rumor that he and manager Gene Mauch were not the best of friends, I called the Expos and worked out a deal for Singleton. The right fielder was a major contributor to the Orioles and for the next ten seasons brought a pocketful of skills, including a left-handed power bat.

After Ken's playing career ended, he turned to television and settled in as a successful baseball play-by-play announcer. Jorgensen later was the Cardinals' director of player development for many years.

Broadcasting Brilliance

Speaking of broadcasters, I have always felt that it was just as important to have good radio and TV announcers working for the club as it was to have good ballplayers. With every game, there were three hours or more to sell the club over radio and TV media outlets. It was, in effect, an ongoing advertisement. "You can't 'pimp' for the product, but you can make it interesting and exciting to be in the park," I used to tell them. Al Harazin, my assistant GM who had worked for me in Baltimore, agreed with this philosophy and the two of us were forever looking for new talent. We needed a lot of sports announcers and the cast was constantly changing. We had some successes and we had our failures.

Having grown up listening to an array of radio broadcasters, I had a pronounced weakness for announcers with that kind of background. Harazin did not. His skills warmed to TV. It was his suggestion that Tim McCarver, then broadcasting for the Philadelphia Phillies, would be a good addition to our New York Mets TV team. "Put him with Ralph Kiner and let them talk baseball and I think we will have a real winner," he promised—and he was 100 percent right. Kiner, the former Pittsburgh home run hitter, had been a TV broadcaster since the expansion National League club appeared in New York.

Tim McCarver was more than just another baseball announcer. His knowledge of the game and its intricacies became obvious. His long career as a Major League catcher for the Cardinals and the Phillies no doubt prepared him for this new role in baseball.

Al Harazin's prediction of matching him with Kiner was uncannily correct. Talking baseball was a real winner—for the Mets at that time and later on national networks.

McCarver, a kid out of Memphis, Tennessee, who was an early fan of fellow townsman Elvis Presley, also loved music. He liked to listen but he also loved to sing. This led to his singing in a musical recording that never got the accolades it deserved.

Knowing that Timmy was proud and respectful of his father, a lawman in Memphis, I sent him a letter of condolences when his dad passed away. McCarver later told me that he kept that letter in his briefcase and read it from time to time. That's the kind of guy Tim McCarver was and is today.

On the radio side with the Mets, Bob Murphy was equally strong, as good as anyone who ever called balls and strikes.

We were never above talking to our Minor League connections about their likes and dislikes about broadcasters in their part of the baseball world. David Rosenfield, the longtime COO and general manager at our Triple-A Norfolk team, was a constant source of information, on both players and announcers. Once, when asked the latter question, he said he liked a young man calling the game in Portland, Maine. "It is his first season in the broadcast booth," he reported. "I'm not sure how he got the job, because he is also the team lawyer and I understand he has a share of the ownership." Intrigued, we got a sample of the young man's work from the radio station, then offered him a job. He accepted, and thus Gary Thorn came to work for the Mets. When a local newspaper media columnist asked how we could bring to New York an announcer who had spent only a single season in the Minors, my reply was that the New York sports audience was probably the most discerning in the world and we would know in short order whether our decision had been right. Thorn went on to become one of the outstanding announcers in the country.

Things didn't always go our way. Even though our intentions were good and the talent was evident, we didn't always get our man. Example number one was that of a young radio sports reporter out of St. Louis who seemed to be extremely conversant with baseball and looked to us to be ready for the big leagues. We got in touch and invited him to New York for an interview.

Several days later, Al and I met the young man, Bob Costas, for breakfast at the New York Athletic Club. It was an easy interview. Bob professed his love for the game and that he had always dreamed of doing play-by-play. He apparently was enthralled with Mickey Mantle, and that occupied a goodly part of our conversation. We did not discuss salary but told him we would be happy to have him with the Mets. He seemed pleased with the meeting and said he would get back to us shortly. He then said that NBC had wanted to talk with him and that because he was going to be in New York had set up a meeting with the television giant that afternoon. Harazin and I left the Athletic Club convinced we had added a bright young man to our announcer team. How { 149 wrong we were! The next morning Costas phoned and said that NBC had made him an offer he couldn't refuse. He thanked us profusely and sincerely for our offer, and we wished him all the best luck in his endeavors with the national network.

The other case that comes to mind was more like love's labor lost. Jack Buck and his wife, Carol, were good friends of mine and constant companions when I went to Ireland as the guest of Mike Roarty, the senior vice president of Anheuser-Busch, which sponsored the Irish Derby, one of the world's top horse races.

Jack was a crack play-by-play announcer for St. Louis in both football and baseball. The Bucks had a son in college at Indiana University, who already was doing some of the play-by-play for the Cardinals. He filled in for his father but worked independently, too, and Mike Roarty told me that Joe Buck had all the earmarks of a great announcer. I heard him work, and I was impressed.

When I returned to New York, I told Al Harazin that we should and could have young Joe, who would be an instant upgrade to our media group, and that he was only raw talent who would be getting better every year. Harazin thought about my suggestion overnight and came back with the following question: "Frank, do you think you may be thinking with your heart and not your head? I know his parents are good friends with you and your wife, and is that why you rate their son so highly?"

Al's caution hit me hard. Although I didn't necessarily believe that, Al's question was fair. Frankly, I wasn't sure, and although the final decision was mine, I didn't argue the point further and dropped the idea. What a mistake. In short order, Joe Buck landed a steady job with the Cardinals, following in his father's footsteps, and soon after, at age twenty-five, was hired by the Fox Network to do both football and baseball, where he has excelled ever since.

My experience dealing with broadcasters had come early. When Jerry Hoffberger tapped me to be advertising director of National Brewing, my duties included dealing with the media rights to 150 } the Baltimore Orioles and the Baltimore Colts. Our brewery held primary broadcasting rights to both franchises, including hiring the play-by-play and what was known as the "color man." That included both radio and TV. Already under contract with National Brewing were Chuck Thompson and Bailey Goss, both as talented in their specialties as virtually anyone in the country. Thompson, a tall, rail-thin Pennsylvania native, excelled at play-by-play; and Goss, a well-built handsome gent, did outstanding commercial work.

True, we struck out on some, but we scored home runs on others in Baltimore. Frank Messer, whom we tracked down in Richmond, Virginia, broadcast in Baltimore before moving onto the New York Yankees. Another first was Jim Karvellas, a local guy, and Bill O'Donnell came out of Syracuse, New York, to rank with Thompson as perhaps the best team of play-by-play announcers the O's ever produced.

Thompson was absolutely the top individual talent we ever put on the air. He could make the call as clearly and concisely as any working guy. For him, the ball was always hit to a position and fielded by an individual. Thus, the radio listener knew exactly what was happening as it happened. The color comments came later.

For example, here's the ideal description of a play for radio: "It's a hard grounder to short; Cal Ripken is up with it and fires to first, in time." The listener gets the essentials as they're happening and in conjunction with the crowd noise. Then, the broadcaster would review the play, with more description and color: "Ripken had to go far to his right, threw off balance, but got the runner by two steps."

We encouraged our broadcasters to develop their own signature home-run call. Chuck Thompson had two unique lines to indicate a round-tripper: "Ain't the beer cold!" and "Go to war, Miss Agnes." Phil Rizzuto, who did Yankee play-by-play, made famous "Holy Cow," as did Harry Caray. Caray, who broadcast first for the Cardinals, then the A's and the White Sox, and later, more famously, for the Cubbies, had an unforgettable one: "It might be, it could be . . . it is . . . a home run!" Other home-run lines among various broadcasters include "Bye-bye, it's outta here!"; "So long!"; "It's gone!"; "See you later!"; "Kiss that one good-bye!" Baseball Hall of Famer Harry Heilmann, who did play-by-play for the Detroit Tigers in the 1940s, had a distinctive call: "Trouble, trouble, trouble—it's a home run!"

Personally, I thought Jack Buck in his time was the best in the country. Chuck Thompson in Baltimore was probably his equal in calling baseball and football games. Vin Scully in Brooklyn and later Los Angeles is also at the top of my list. But Jack Buck was also the best after-dinner speaker and master of ceremonies I ever witnessed.

Chuck Thompson also had the dubious distinction of doing play-by-play of a plane crash. It happened after a Colts game in Baltimore Memorial Stadium. Tom Davis was finalizing the postgame comments when he spotted a small plane on a descent path for the stadium's upper deck. He immediately turned it over to Chuck, who had just finished calling the football game. In his

{ 151 }

excellent professional way, he described the impending crash and the pilot's escape from the downed plane.

As much involvement as I had in hiring broadcasters, I rarely appeared on game broadcasts. That changed somewhat in my final years with the Mets and it was not unusual to hear me step in, when needed, and work color commentary with the play-by-play man. In fact, in my last year with the New York club and the final game of the season, playing the Phillies in Philadelphia, I worked with Ralph Kiner. He called the game and I backed him as the "color man." It didn't happen often, just once in a while.

Much earlier, while I was still a sportswriter at the *Baltimore News-Post*, I was hired to do a daily sports show, Monday through Friday, on Baltimore's WITH. It meant extra dollars, and you never turned down the opportunity for more money. But the newspaper objected. The *News-Post* claimed that it owned the name "Frank Cashen" because of my writing daily bylined stories in its paper and that I could not use that name on radio. This was before television had caught hold, and there was a natural rivalry between newspapers and the radio in covering the news.

Someone suggested that I do the radio stint under another name, and both the station and the paper somewhat reluctantly agreed. I came up with the name "Frank Ryan," Ryan being my mother's maiden name, and the *Frank Ryan Scholastic Sports Show* took off. We got some sponsors and the show lasted about a year and a half until it became impossible to do a five-days-a-week radio deal while traveling and writing for the newspaper. It had been a constant struggle to serve two masters but I never regretted having the experience. Eventually, the *News-Post* backed off its position of "owning" names, and two of my old cohorts, John Steadman, later sports editor, and Neal Eskridge, a writer, both had successful daily radio shows while still working for the paper.

The *Sun* newspapers were the other major Baltimore competition at the time, and word emerged that the *Sun* had purchased a new item known as a television franchise and that it would be part of the CBS Network. Searching for talent to get its franchise started, the *Sun* invited a host of the newspapers' employees to have studio auditions. Some of the invitees were delighted with the opportunity and others were something less than happy. Among the latter was a good friend of mine, Jim McManus, a *Sun* reporter who covered a police beat and had recently been given a permanent assignment to one of the well-defined police districts. On the day he was to be interviewed by the TV people, Jim told me over lunch it was a waste of time because he had worked a couple of years to get his new assignment and had no interest in the TV business.

Jim had graduated from Baltimore's Loyola College a few years ahead of me, and he also had worked for the school newspaper, the *Greyhound*, and was particularly interested in sports. He also was married to a neat gal, Margaret Dempsey, who was one of the top writers at the *Sun*. He and I often kidded that if you added our two IQS, it would still not be as high as Margaret's.

You know, of course, what happened. He came out of that 1947 interview with a firm offer from the TV people, and finally, at the urging of the editorial people at the *Sun*, he joined WMAR-TV. His was the first voice heard in Baltimore on local TV. It didn't take long for the TV bunch to recognize McManus's obvious talent. In shorter order, he was heading up the afternoon variety show, the station's best offering. Jim was also a natural on any of the news or sports shows and could fit in anyplace WMAR had a need. It became clear that he could do it all, and the networks in New York came a-calling years later.

CBS, the parent of the local station, had first crack at his services but they had an unusual condition, not unusual to Frank "Ryan" Cashen but unusual nonetheless. The network wanted to change his name to Jim McKay to head up a variety show they had planned to be called *The Real McKay*. That switch went through without a hitch. Sports became his specialty from then on, and after a brief fling at NBC, ABC became his network of choice, where his *Wide World of Sports* show ran for thirty-seven years.

{ 153

In that range of years, he covered all manner and means of sports. To me, it was his considerable work in covering twelve Olympics that stood out, particularly, the Munich massacre in 1972 when he covered not only the games but also the tragic kidnapping and eventual deaths of the Israeli Olympians. McKay was on the air for fourteen straight hours and brought this tragic story, in a timely but compassionate way, to viewers all over the world.

While working in New York, I came across McKay on frequent occasions and I was delighted when we both were selected for the Loyola College Hall of Fame at the same time.

As for my own brief time behind the mike, I enjoyed doing the sports show back in Baltimore and the occasional "color" visit to the Mets broadcast booth, but it was not my forte.

27

New Friends, New Places

I never had a job I didn't like and I've had quite a few, going back
to the beginning in the newspaper business. I was well satisfied and quite happy moving to race tracks and then to the beer
business, which brought new challenges that didn't upset me a
bit. Particularly, I loved the advertising game. Still, getting into
baseball was a joyous leap.

One of the results of this kind of serendipitous journey was
meeting so many different kinds of people. Take, for instance,
the beer business. I was lucky because Hoffberger took me to
the annual beer business meetings and I saw the giants of that
industry at their best. The top guy in the business was August A.
Busch Jr. of Anheuser-Busch, the St. Louis patriarch of the German family that owned the Budweiser brewery. He had been at
it longer than the rest of us, and when he spoke we all paid close
attention. Gussie, as he was known, ruled with an iron hand and
headed the largest and most successful operation in the business.

Busch had bought the St. Louis Cardinals in 1953, and thus,
Jerry Hoffberger was the second owner to simultaneously run a
brewery and a ball club. Busch's oldest son eventually eased the
old man out of the beer business but left the Cardinals in Gussie's
hands. One of the stories of the latter, which always amused me,
came about when Gussie mentioned to his successful baseball
manager Whitey Herzog that he was thinking about giving him a
lifetime contract. To which Herzog was reported to have replied:

{ 155

"Whose lifetime are we talking about, Mr. Busch, yours or mine?" Despite good intentions, such a contract never came about.

Some of Busch's disciples became cherished friends of mine, none more so than Mike Roarty, who headed marketing at Anheuser-Busch. Mike did a lot of things I had done at National Brewery but, of course, on a much larger scale. The first time I met Mike was in San Diego when I was there for some baseball business and he was preaching the gospel of Anheuser-Busch. As we were both first-generation Irish Americans, we quickly decided to seal our newly found friendship with some Irish whiskey. None being available, Mike sent one of his aides in pursuit of a bottle of same. And somehow the aide finally returned with a bottle of Jameson, a popular Irish whiskey. The two of us sat down to satisfy our thirst. Somewhere in the middle of the set-to, we agreed not to quit until the bottle was empty. After reaching that goal, we parted, staggering somewhat, with the promise that we would get back together in the not-too-distant future.

156 }

Since Budweiser was one of the principal sponsors of the New York Mets on radio and television, it was relatively easy for me to go along with a host of Roarty's marketing ideas. With his brewery sponsoring the Irish Derby, staged at the Curragh Racecourse outside Dublin and one of the prestigious thoroughbred horse races in the world, Mike led a group of us to Dublin every year to be in attendance. He leased a castle, Luttrellstown, on the outskirts of Dublin, each year to house us for the week or more we'd be spending in Ireland.

Anheuser-Busch, the gigantic American brewery that was seeking to expand its business into Europe, had taken over sponsorship of the race and it had become known as the Budweiser Irish Derby, named after the brewery's flagship beer brand.

My friend Mike Roarty headed up the marketing team for the newly sponsored run. And, as I previously mentioned, every year he put together a traveling party of sports figures, Hollywood people, and various VIPs and took us overseas for the festivities that surrounded the race. Once in Ireland, we were joined by local bigwigs and a slate of national officials.

A skilled after-dinner speaker who was also known to break out in song when called upon, Roarty loved to party and he kept that in mind when he put together the traveling crew. Luttrellstown Castle, a fourteen-bedroom-suite beauty, was our headquarters in Dublin, and Jean and I somehow got to be a permanent part of the travel bunch. There was a very good Irish piano player on hand every evening and that was the starting point for the nightly party—or, at the very least, a dinner party.

Among the Hollywood types who were regulars on the annual Irish junket were Gene Autry, the legendary Hollywood cowboy; Donald O'Connor, the song and dance man; John Forsyth, the longtime star of TV's *Dynasty*; and Norm Crosby, the double-talking perennial favorite entertainer. Singer Tony Bennett, who came just once in the fading days of our odysseys, left his mark and it was a distinctive one. If the evenings were made for singing, Tony's days were made for painting, serious painting, eye-filling painting. There are people much smarter than me who claim Tony could have made a comfortable living as a professional painter, and I saw nothing to contradict these evaluations. { 157

From Day One at the castle we began to prepare for a lavish party we would stage for the local dignitaries before vacating the castle. It was my responsibility to weave the Hollywood regulars into a stage show that featured Mike Roarty as the closing act. Tony Bennett, who sang in our final closing stage show, was one of my favorites. Donald O'Connor established a chorus line for the ladies and choreographed the necessary steps. With repeated hours of practice, the ladies took their efforts at show business very seriously. And to tell the truth, they were actually very good.

For me it was a constant chore of juggling the Irish Derby and our bi-yearly golf tours, but they were only minor struggles compared to fitting Ireland into the middle of baseball season. Then, too, Mike and a certain few of us would sometimes leave

Dublin after the Irish Derby and fly to London for the Wimbledon tennis classic where we were hosted by NBC, which had a large tent inside the stadium grounds. The tent was filled with great food and drink, including a large share of Wimbledon's signature dish, strawberries and cream.

When we were at Wimbledon on the Fourth of July, some lusty singing broke out at the NBC tent. "God Bless America" was probably the longest presentation, but several others, like "My Country 'Tis of Thee," were less vocal. Somebody suggested that was because fewer of the Americans knew the words. The British seemed to be less entertained by it all but kept their heads up and their voices down and generally handled the matter with quiet grace.

Suffice it to say that these Ireland trips were great experiences, fun times, the kind you will always remember. Like winning baseball pennants, they were too good ever to forget. The Irish Derby guest list each year had included the aforementioned Hollywood people, a lesser group of sports names, and a mixed batch from other pursuits. My favorite among the latter was an ex-marine officer and a highly successful beer distributor from Tampa, Florida, Artie Pepin, and his wife, Polly. Among his other accomplishments, Artie was the oldest patient ever to receive a heart transplant. History had it that Artie was on the soon-to-die list in a Houston heart hospital when he got a new heart that had previously belonged to a twenty-five-year-old Texas construction worker who had been killed in a motorcycle accident. Now having a twenty-five-year-old heart, Pepin decided to live like it, and as far as I am concerned, he achieved that goal.

Artie, who was an unusually good friend of Gussie Busch, had put together a successful and thriving beer distributorship in Gainesville, Florida, many years before. One day he got a telephone call from Gussie's office, informing him that the big boss would like to see him in St. Louis as soon as possible. When Artie arrived at headquarters, he was told that Busch would like to take back the distributorship in Gainesville, but in exchange Artie could have any vacant territory in the United States. With great reluctance, but in the spirit of their personal friendship, Artie agreed to Gussie's wish, and to complete the deal he selected Tampa as the location of his new endeavor. He was then offered the neighboring St. Petersburg territory as well but declined the extra geography and reported that the Tampa market alone would be sufficient. That done, the irrepressible Pepin began to build what turned out to be one of the most successful beer franchises in the world.

Artie told me that when he asked Mr. Busch what the secret was behind the request for him to give up the Gainesville territory, he was told that the Cardinal baseball team had a chance of signing free agent Yankee slugger Roger Maris, who had broken Babe Ruth's coveted home run record. One of the paramount things Maris had demanded was the Budweiser distributorship in Gainesville. He signed with the Cards after getting exactly { 159 what he had requested. Maris got Gainesville, Gussie got Maris, and Artie got Tampa.

One of my other favorites on the Irish trips was the afore-mentioned Gene Autry. Of course, he was widely known as the "Singing Cowboy" in films from the 1930s through the 1950s. Gene also was the controlling stakeholder in the California Angels baseball team from 1961 to 1995. The Angels went through a series of name changes—from California Angels to Los Angeles Angels to Los Angeles Angels at Anaheim. Gene was much beloved by Angels fans. When the team won its first and only World Series in 2002, after Gene's death in 1998, banners proclaimed, "This One's for Gene."

I first met Gene, born Orvon Grover Autry, in 1966 when the Orioles squared off in the World Series against the LA Dodgers. As the local owner of the American League Angels, Autry called and said he would help with hotel arrangements and introduce us to Los Angeles. That began a friendship that lasted over many years. I saw Autry often and we enjoyed socializing together—

whether in a bar or restaurant or on trips to the Irish Derby with Mike Roarty. When Gene's first wife died, he married a younger woman who was a loan officer at a local bank where Autry did business. This prompted a famous headline in a tabloid newspaper: "Cowboy Marries Loan Arranger." Gene tried to persuade me to join him with the Angels as general manager but I opted to stay in the East. Gene and his new wife flew all the way across the country to attend my retirement party from the Mets in 1992. Donald O'Conner and his wife also came from California to New York for the same festivities.

Another Californian I got to know after he had pulled off his New York uniform was Joe DiMaggio, the Yankee Clipper. After he retired, Joe was on the board of the Orioles, then owned by Edward Bennett Williams, the noted Washington lawyer who also owned part of the Washington Redskins football team. Williams had bought the Orioles from Jerry Hoffberger in 1980.

160 }

During that time, Joe and I developed a friendship and went to dinner several times over the years. One thing never brought up was the subject of Marilyn Monroe, one of Joe's former wives. If someone brought up Marilyn's name, Joe might just walk out—even in the middle of dinner.

One meeting with DiMaggio was especially memorable. We were both in San Francisco, his hometown, for the 1989 World Series between the Giants and their cross-bay rivals, the Oakland A's. I noticed that DiMaggio was at a nearby table in the press tent before the start of Game Three at San Francisco's Candlestick Park. Joe came over to see me, perhaps fleeing from the press of admirers. Knowing that I had a place in Florida, Joe said he was considering moving there and asked some questions about life in the Sunshine State. Then, right after we chatted, the infamous earthquake that led to a ten-day delay in the World Series shook the stadium. We were all scared to death, not knowing whether the shocks and shaking would worsen. I thought later that I would have been the last guy to see Joe DiMaggio alive.

Another baseball legend I had the privilege of knowing well was Stan Musial, the St. Louis Cardinals star of the 1940s and '50s who compiled a lifetime batting average of .331 and amassed 3,630 hits. Jean and I first met Stan and his devoted wife, Lil, when I was with the Mets and we were included in those annual trips to the Irish Derby.

By the time I knew Stan, he was retired from active playing, but I was very familiar with his athletic achievements. Amazingly, Stan, nicknamed "The Man," hit equally well against both right-handed and left-handed pitchers. He had the same lifetime average against pitching from both sides—a feat I don't think has ever been duplicated.

Musial was fond of playing the harmonica, whether it was in the clubhouse or at social gatherings. He always had the harmonica along with him and we enjoyed some of his serenades during the trips to Ireland. Only problem was that once Stan started playing, you couldn't get him to stop. Harmonica music was not something you wanted to hear all evening. Obviously, Stan enjoyed it, though. He once told me he would rather have been a member of a good band than a ballplayer, but I never believed it for one second. Stan, who grew up in the industrial town of Donora, Pennsylvania, started out as a pitcher, but a sore arm caused him to switch to the outfield. The rest is history.

One morning while Jean and I were attending Hall of Fame induction ceremonies in Cooperstown, New York, Stan greeted my wife, "Jean, Jean, how are you?" When she replied about some ache or pain, Stan responded, "At our age, if we wake up in the morning and don't have any aches and pains, we're dead."

The always-cheerful Musial was noted for greeting people with "Whadayasay? Whadayasay?" Like the harmonica, it was his trademark. When Musial had an audience with the Pope in Rome, one of the other attendees was asked what Stan said to His Holiness. He replied, "Whadayasay, whadayasay, Pope?"

Beloved in St. Louis, Stan was a credit to the game. Unlike so

{ 161

many baseball heroes, Stan was never touched by controversy or scandal. He played the game well and responded to his adoring fans. Fans who were youngsters in St. Louis in the '40s and '50s recall how Stan would sign autographs (for free, then) in the parking lot outside the old Sportsman's Park long after everyone else had departed. He was that kind of a guy.

Certainly one of the most memorable personalities I ever met was the result of a business trip with Jerry Hoffberger back in my days in the advertising business with the brewery. Once a year we traveled to Europe to make a string of commercials. We also got background music for some TV shots and obtained professional talent at competitive rates. After several visits to London, we headed for Brussels, Belgium, to work in a studio principally known as the place where the Singing Nun had recorded a string of hits. And one evening in Brussels turned out to be one of the most interesting of my life.

162 }

But to back up a bit, the world was looking at a potential international catastrophe in October of 1962—the Cuban Missile Crisis. The previous year, President John F. Kennedy had overseen an unsuccessful attempt to invade Cuba. Now the Russians were reportedly shipping missiles to Castro's Cuba. The world was astir!

The night before we were scheduled to leave for Brussels, I was fast asleep in my home in Baltimore County when the phone rang in what could be called "the middle of the night." It was Hoffberger, to tell me that he felt the current political situation made it unwise for us to travel on the same plane and that he had arranged alternate plans for me to get to Europe. By this time, I had all the lights on and wrote down his instructions on my always-ready yellow pad. Jean, who by this time was wide awake, asked the obvious question: Why were we going at all with the international situation so serious? There being no answer, we settled back for a few hours of troubled sleep.

We all made it to Brussels—Hoffberger, Herb Fried, Hank Russell (our creative ad guy), and me. Work went well, and the third or fourth night, Hoffberger invited Herb and me to go to dinner, explaining that a gentleman was flying in from Italy to have some private political talks and that he had cleared us (whatever that meant) to attend.

We arrived at the appointed time and place, at what was obviously a first-class restaurant—an eating club at which our visitor had made arrangements. We were shown to a private room and in short order joined by our host, Emilio Pucci, the world-renowned fashion designer. Pucci, after having started at the University of Milan, got a good part of his education in the United States at the University of Georgia and Reed College in Oregon, where he received a skiing scholarship. He was not only a good skier but also a competitive swimmer, fencer, and exceptional tennis player, and he raced cars and flew airplanes. He had served in the Italian air force during World War II and later established his highly successful, sophisticated clothing business. He numbered among his patrons such luminaries as Jackie Kennedy, Sophia Loren, and, later, Madonna. The legendary Marilyn Monroe was buried in one of his creations.

Hoffberger was deep in politics at this time, having been solidly behind Jack Kennedy in his 1960 run for president. He also was a major player nationally within the Jewish community and an unofficial, but potent, force on the political scene. So it was not a great stretch of the imagination to realize that this meeting with Pucci had something to do with international politics.

Pucci was short, almost a small man, elegantly dressed. He was wearing a large homburg, which he took off as he entered the room. His black overcoat reached down well below his knees. When he took off the coat, a stunning dark suit was revealed, giving one the impression that it was made by the best of the Italian tailors. Pucci spent some time making the three of us feel at ease. As I remember, his English was flawless and he never seemed to reach for a word or a phrase. I watched in naive silence as he asked the maître d' for a wine list. I knew we were in for an exceptional time.

The whole evening was a two-way dialogue between Hoffberger and Pucci, which, for me, was like watching a tennis match. I enjoyed it immensely and kept my mouth shut.

To sum up, the conversation between the two titans went like this: Pucci (obviously heavy into Italian politics) said that he and many of his political allies felt that the Italian Communist Party was on the verge of taking over Italy. Things had been going in that direction, and he and his friends were fearful that the end was near. He didn't think President Kennedy was aware of the depth of the political problem in Italy, and he implored Hoffberger to advise the president personally of their fears. As he continued to paint a bleak picture, Pucci startled me with the revelation that he and his allies had an airplane on standby at a private site near Rome to fly Pope John XXIII out of the country before the Communists took over the Vatican. Move the Pope out of Rome! That possibility shattered me. And Hoffberger was to explain all of this to Kennedy.

Several important questions were asked. Some were answered by Pucci; to others, there were no answers. Where would they take the Pope when he left Rome? The answer was "Ireland." What happens if the Pope refuses to leave? For that Pucci had no answer, other than to say, "We will see." "Would you, could you, take him by force?" Hoffberger asked. "We will see, we will see," Pucci repeated. I have replayed that night in my mind for more than fifty years. They would rescue the Pope and move him from Rome to Ireland? Did the Italians have a deal with the Swiss guards who are pledged to guard the Pope and the Papacy with their lives? The questions still abound and the answers are still bewildering.

Hoffberger had asked our Italian host to order the meal for the group. It was a fortunate request and the results were truly fabulous. We parted amid handshakes and smiles—a check never appeared. Hoffberger later told me that he had given the details to President Kennedy. Fortunately, the Communists did not take over in Italy, and the whole scenario, so painfully discussed that evening, never played out.

28

Traveling Tales

Sometimes because the job dictated it and other times because the invitations were too compelling to resist, I did a lot of traveling.

Baseball was the number one reason. Just following those Oriole teams of the late '60s and '70s and later with the Mets got me around the length and breadth of the United States—from Boston to LA and Seattle to Florida. Mexico, a source of player talent and MLB meetings, and Canada, which had MLB teams in Toronto and Montreal, were part of the annual routine as well as Puerto Rico and winter ball in South America.

During my time in the commissioner's office, I was sent to Venezuela to negotiate winter ball contracts. Upon my arrival at the Caracas airport, among the first sights were heavily armed guards. The whole scene left me unsettled and I was tempted to catch the next flight back to New York. I only had come to negotiate baseball contracts and would leave as soon as that was accomplished. But on second thought, I decided to keep my mouth shut and see where it would lead me. The answer to that came shortly.

I went to airport customs and offered my passport. After the usual questions as to where I was born and so forth, the gentleman, if I may call him that, on the other side of the glass slipped my passport into a nearby desk drawer and told me it would be returned when I was leaving the country. Now I became visibly upset. I had been instructed to never give up my passport at any time or for any reason.

Fortunately, there was a group of Venezuelan baseball people who had come to welcome me to their country and to serve as tour guides. Recognizing my obvious unhappiness, they inserted themselves into the conversation and assured me this was the law of the land and that my passport was in safe hands and, as promised, would be returned when I left the country. Three days later after we had concluded our discussions, the baseball people returned me to the airport and I retrieved my passport and flew safely back to New York.

Three times baseball has taken me to Japan, and they were all enjoyable journeys. American-style baseball is almost like a religion in Japan, and American visitors to that country are treated with great respect.

My first trip was in October of 1971, when the Orioles were invited to spend up to a month playing in eighteen exhibition games against Japanese clubs throughout that country. This trip came soon after our hard-fought loss to the Pirates in the World Series. There was some money in the deal for the players, and owner Jerry Hoffberger of the O's had no objections, so the negotiations intensified. Having no interest in going with less than a complete ball club, as the chief executive, I told the Oriole team that the proposed trip, which included full rides for players' wives and similar accommodations for the remainder of the traveling party, would be put to a vote by the players. But, I warned, anything less than a unanimous approval vote would cancel the venture. We later learned that the few would-be "no" votes were heavily influenced by the other ladies and in short order we had a unanimous positive verdict. This, of course, was before such an extracurricular activity would have been subject to review by the MLB Players Association.

The charter flight to Japan started in Baltimore, stopped in San Francisco to pick up additional players and their wives, and flew then to Honolulu and eventually to Tokyo. As someone who made that entire twenty-hour-plus trip, I can tell you that the arriving plane looked like it had been the scene of a giant sleepover, with pillows and blankets generously settled through the cabin along with the remains of several large cocktail parties. The principal topic of conversation at this point had to do with the number of Bloody Marys that Boog Powell had consumed during the plane ride.

Alice and Jerry Hoffberger had flown in for the first game and the opening ceremonies as the Orioles took on the Yomiuri Giants, the number one team in Japan. As part of the opening ceremonies, the top representative of the visiting club was given a traditional "presento," or gift, by the home team. The Hoffbergers were, of course, on hand to receive the "presento," which at that time and for the rest of the trip turned out to be a valued electronics gift. These gifts included TV sets of every conceivable size, music boxes, dictating equipment, and the like. The Hoffbergers, off on a lengthy tourist trip in the Far East, flew out the very next day and left the remainder of the trip in the hands of the staff.   { 167

The "presentos" through the remaining stops went to my wife and me, and at trip's end we were overwhelmed with how to get the "presentos" back to the United States. Our clubhouse man came up with the solution. The Japanese coveted the American wooden bats, so he suggested we give the remaining lumber to the Japanese teams and use the empty bat trunks to send all of those gifts to Baltimore. The trip went well from a baseball standpoint, too. The Orioles played like the champions they were and crowd receptions were warm everywhere we went. The lone problem came when we were packing to go home and three of the entourage, two ballplayers and one staff member, had designs on staying in Japan with newfound female friends. Cooler heads prevailed, and with the urging of their teammates we all got out of Japan on time, leaving a job well done.

Some of the old cultural customs were still in force in Japan during that 1971 visit. For instance, wives did not accompany their husbands on social or business occasions. Thus, the Japanese ballplayers' wives never got a chance to meet their American counterparts, a decision that left both sides unhappy. If there was any sort of need for females, the roles were filled by geisha, young ladies properly schooled to handle and wait on invited guests.

By the time I got back to Japan for another all-star tour in 1979, social changes were under way. The most obvious change was in women's clothing. Kimonos were all but gone. The country had discovered denim, at least as far as young people were concerned. Denim slacks, denim skirts, denim jackets were everywhere and signaled more changes to come. Women were being absorbed into the work force and flooded the downtown streets, nearly all of them dressed in identical somber gray suits and white blouses. Then, too, they began to accompany their husbands on social occasions, and the interaction between their team and the U.S. squad was instantaneous. It was evident that the Japanese wives were anxious to learn from their American counterparts, and fashion appeared to be the prime discussion matter. As previously mentioned, there were two all-star teams touring the country, a team of National Leaguers and an American League squad. The tour had been arranged by the commissioner's office and I was leading the tour. The games were well played and drew big crowds. I don't remember which all-star team prevailed, but the scores were secondary to the goodwill it brought for American baseball.

My third visit to Japan came several years later when the country staged what it called a baseball summit, in which the American game was examined from the Little Leagues to the Big League and everything in between. I was selected as one of the major presenters, and my topic was "How to Build a Big League Club." I had been allotted two hours for my presentation and I had to dig deep to come up with enough material. What I hadn't anticipated was that a Japanese translator had been assigned to the project, and as I was making my presentation in English, he was repeating the same in Japanese to the largely native attendees. The entire presentation took just under five hours and was judged a success by the people who had put the program together.

Closing out the festivities was a mammoth party and banquet and the Japanese brought the singer and actress Diana Ross over from the States to head the entertainment. Formal clothes were the dress for the numerous Japanese women, and Jean informed me that the frocks came from the best dressmakers in London, Rome, Paris, and New York. They were, in a word, dazzling.

History has it that baseball came to Japan in the 1880s from two different sources, one a teacher and the other a student. In 1872 Horace Wilson, an American teaching in Japan, decided to include an American sport, baseball, in his curriculum, and thus began the slow growth of the game. Six years later, a Japanese student, schooled in the United States, returned to his homeland having developed a passion for the game and anxious to see it prosper in Japan. He worked diligently to that end. From whatever the source, the Japanese saw the game as largely physical, and their players trained each day until they were exhausted. This left the fitness of the teams, especially the pitchers, somewhat suspect, but it was from overtraining rather than the opposite.

The professional phase of the sport did not arrive until 1930 and it hasn't stopped since. Babe Ruth drew huge crowds when he and other American ballplayers made a barnstorming trip to Japan in 1934. The Japanese major leagues mimicked the U.S. game in every way. As in the United States, there are two major leagues, the Central and the Pacific. Their official season is 144 games, versus 162 in the States, with a playoff between the two leagues producing a national champion.

Written agreements between the two countries now provide for U.S. players to work in the Japanese leagues and Japanese players to participate in the U.S. Major Leagues. Players from the South American countries and other nations around the world also are welcomed by both nations, and that overused title of "world champions" is getting ever closer to being a legitimate boast.

By the time of my last trip to Japan, the physical size of the Japanese players had changed. When we first visited there in 1971, the players, to my eye, appeared smallish at five feet three or four and certainly outsized by the visiting Americans. In just a few years, the average was something like five eight or five nine, and six-footers were not uncommon. Most baseball players I spoke to attributed the size increase to the changing diet—with less rice and more meat, fish, dairy products, and vegetables—that the country had switched to after World War II.

Along with the increase in physical stature, there seemed to be a similar improvement in baseball skills. The result, of course, was that U.S. Major League teams started to scout their friends across the Pacific, and thus began a parade of Japanese players to America beginning in the mid-1990s. It was with Japan's permission, of course, but it goes without saying that it was the cream of the crop. Players like Ichiro Suzuki, Hiroki Kuroba, Yu Darvish, Daisuke Matsuzaka, and Hideki Matsui have excelled in the U.S. Majors. The march started as one-by-one, but the ones began to add up quickly. Then the march began to reverse, slowly but surely, as the U.S. players, and particularly their agents, learned there were opportunities across the Pacific and a number of older U.S. players switched over. These moves seemed minor at the time, but the talk about a "real World Series" began to be heard even outside Japan.

When the World Baseball Classic was developed, the fact that Japan won the first two championships (and finished second to the Dominican Republic in the third) of what has become a regular and popular international event is further testimony to the baseball progress of that nation, and a true World Series may be in the offing someday. But few are willing to estimate when "someday" would be.

Prior to my baseball sojourns to Japan, brewery business took me to various spots in Europe, including Belgium, England, and France. Personally, my favorite destinations were Italy and Ireland.

My initial visit to Italy was almost by chance. Several years earlier I had been the featured speaker at a dinner honoring the top officers of Pan American Airways, and as an "honorarium," I was presented with two first-class, round-trip passes to any place Pan Am flew. These passes sat around our home for a couple of years and were barely discussed. Then suddenly I read that Pan Am was seriously considering closing down. That brought to mind those two valued passes, and a serious discussion with my wife, Jean, revealed she would like to go to Italy, which we had never visited. The baseball season was recently concluded and we were free to go wherever we desired.

A simple phone call lined up two seats on a Pan Am flight from JFK Airport to Rome. I spent a couple of days lining up hotels and Italian train reservations and we were off on the journey. Not more than twenty minutes into the flight, an announcement came out of the cockpit identifying the flight, the destination, and the name of the senior pilot, Frank White. "A fairly common name," I assured my wife, "but I think I know that pilot." I briefly explained to Jean, and calling over the nearest flight attendant, I requested that at an appropriate time would she approach the pilot to reveal that one of the passengers, Frank Cashen, had asked if he had played lacrosse at St. Paul's Prep School in Baltimore and then at Johns Hopkins University before joining Pan Am.

An encouraging smile was all we got from the flight attendant but nothing in the way of a comment after she emerged from the cockpit. Shortly thereafter came word that the plane had reached a certain flying level, and the captain, an ex-lacrosse player, reached our seat and we began to discuss old acquaintances. Reaching back in memory, I recalled that White had gotten his first flying experience in the service, loved it, and then became a professional pilot when he returned to civilian status. After that short but spirited discussion, we agreed to reunite when we got to Rome for dinner that same night.

Italy, particularly Rome, was full of wonders, and Jean and I never walked as much in our lives as we did there. We left the hotel in the morning and were afoot from one historic gem to another, not returning to the hotel until early evening in time to freshen up and take off for one of the many interesting restaurants.

But Rome was only the start of it. Jean had booked us on a train north to Florence, where we spent four or five days doing the museums, including one full day visiting with Michelangelo's famous *David*. Not willing to spend too much time in any one place, next it was on the train again, this time to Venice, which we visited hurriedly before returning to Rome and the Pan Am flight back to New York.

The scenario for our second trip to Italy was vastly different. With two other couples of our oldest and best friends, we flew in to Switzerland and then trained through the Alps to Lake Como in Italy. A journey halfway around that lake brings you to Bellagio, a beautiful resort, and after another five days we returned to the town of Como, from which we trained to the Italian fashion headquarters in Milan. Rather than clothes, we picked up a six-passenger van in Milan and headed off to beautiful Tuscany, where we rented a villa for a three-week stay. Motoring out virtually every day, we visited historic towns in the area and finally left Tuscany for a few days in Rome before flying home.

We learned one thing for certain during that visit to Tuscany. If you stick to the small restaurants, the trattorias, where the papa is out front looking after the customers and serving his homemade wine and mama is in the kitchen, turning out those delicious home-made meals, you can't miss. Occasionally, the roles were reversed with the female out front and the father in the back but the result is still first-class. The only failures, at least as far as far as I was concerned, were the large establishments that promised French cooking with high-sounding names. Basically, in Italy, they are frauds.

My favorite overseas destination was, and still is, Ireland. The fact that my mother and father, Bridget and Con Cashen, both were born in County Tipperary and I have close relatives sprinkled throughout the country may have something to do with my preference.

Back when I was still short of my tenth birthday, Bridget and Con had taken the family to Ireland to meet with their parents, our grandparents, and a virtual army of relatives on both sides of the family tree. Riding the daily donkey-pulled cart with milk to the local creamery and rounding up the stubborn cattle at my mother's ancient family home are two memories I carried from that visit.

It was 1964 before I got back to the "Old Sod." Brewery work in Europe was just finishing up and I elected to stop in Ireland on my way home and visit my mother's sister, Aunt Mary, who was married and lived up in the Silver Mines area in the far reaches of Tipperary. It was to be a short stay, for Thanksgiving was a few days away and I had been given specific orders from my bride that I "better be home by then." Aunt Mary had neither electric power nor indoor plumbing at this time, although the first signs of modernity were evident when the locals talked excitedly about short-wave radios that signaled power in the vicinity.

The typical Irish weather, cold and damp, prevailed, but since I was the first overseas visitor in some time, the locals decided on an old-fashioned house party to honor the visitor. Families arrived from far and near, most carrying covered dishes of food. A large fireplace made Aunt Mary's place comfortable, and I was assigned a seat up close to the fire where the older folks were gathered. Early on I had been offered a drink, which I gratefully accepted. Asked how I took my whiskey, I resolved to inform them, "With water." What came back was a glass full of Irish whiskey with a couple drops of water on top. Sipping that powerful concoction near the blistering fire had me close to reeling. I told myself again what I had previously self-counseled: that I could not, absolutely, show any signs of being affected by the booze—nothing that would embarrass my mother and dad and the U.S. branch of the Cashens when Bridget got the next letter from sister Mary.

Fortunately, I soon had the need to visit the bathroom and since there was no such room for that purpose, I was directed out the back door to a nearby clump of bushes. That cold wind off the Atlantic Ocean hit me then and I felt as if I was frozen stiff. That was the bad news. The good news: it instantly sobered me up. I left Ireland with high regard for the modern conveniences in what my mother and father referred to as "the new world."

Later trips to Ireland would center around golf and horse racing. I had become a very serious golfer after my high school and college experiences as a caddy. There were no such things as golf carts at that time and even the practitioners of that noble game had, at Hillandale Country Club in Baltimore when I was working there, either had to use a caddy or tote the golf bag themselves. The caddy business was brisk, especially on weekends.

Although still very much learning the game while in high school, I filled in on the varsity team. I say "filled in" because there was no other way to quite describe it. Three golfers were regulars on the four-man squad and the coach's quest for that fourth player seemed to go on endlessly. My enthusiasm for the game seemed to improve with every passing year even if my consistency never did.

174 }

Many years later after hearing great things about the Irish golf courses, I talked three of my local colleagues into joining me on a two-week tour. It was a huge success in every way; the weather was good with little rain, the golf courses spectacular, the food and drink surprisingly good. There was no fault to be found with the accommodations and the friendly locals went out of their way to be helpful. We had learned that May, June, or September would be the appropriate time for our venture. During July and August the island was filled to overflowing with tourists and golf courses were jammed. While on the flight home, we started making plans to return two years hence.

Our tales of wonder caused an increasing number of golfers to seek entry on the next trip and the traveling party was set at eight, two foursomes of golfers and a handy number for travel and hotel. That plan lasted for eight more years, in two-year increments, and I'll never forget the details of our final golf trip in 2001.

We had just finished playing the new Old Head Golf Course,

which is on a peninsula stretching out into the Irish Sea on the Irish east coast. We were carrying our clubs back to the bus when a man came out of the clubhouse and, in a loud voice that was almost a bellow, cried, "Yanks, Yanks, you better get in here; they are bombing New York!"

We were inside shortly and watched CNN's TV coverage of the 9/11 calamity. It was three or four hours later when we returned to the hotel and continued to watch CNN's nonstop coverage. Little was known at this time of the cause of the disaster or the who and the why. Two of us had daughters who worked in New York in the vicinity of the World Trade towers, and we continued to try to get through on the few available phone lines to the States. Finally, we were rewarded with good news: both our daughters were safe and sound, had not been involved in the tragedy in lower Manhattan, and had checked in with relatives in other parts of the country.

With airports everywhere in the world in a shutdown mode, our eight-man golf party kept vigil in Ireland. If you had to be marooned any place on the globe, Ireland was not a bad alternative. The Irish people were very understanding, helpful, and gracious. It was the odd native who didn't have some relatives across the Atlantic in America. As a matter of fact, two days after that infamous 9/11 attack, Ireland staged a "Day of Mourning," in which businesses and the bars were closed down and church services prevailed throughout the country.

I had only one airline experience where I feared I might not survive. It happened back in my advertising days in the '60s, on a flight with my friend and ad agency guy Herb Fried. Our journey that morning from Baltimore was to take us to Detroit for a half day of work and then to cross the river to Windsor, Ontario, to catch another flight to Toronto.

As had been my custom when I traveled away from home for more than two or three days, I took Jean out to dinner the night before departure. This was no exception and we ate very well. But I also drank very well. After ordering a National Premium beer and turning it so that any prying eyes could clearly identify it, I drank too many water glasses with the patented ice cubes and a modicum of good scotch whiskey. After three or four of these, the National Premium made an excellent chaser. I only write this down because, walking into the airport the next morning with half a hangover, I noticed one of those insurance machines that peppered every airport at that time. I had to stop, of course, and bought the maximum amount of coverage available. If for nothing else, it seemed to help my hangover.

Sitting up in the front of the plane, Herb and I had just finished a post-breakfast snack when the two stewardesses in the first cabin were summoned to the cockpit. They walked out a short time thereafter looking anything but happy. One of the ladies disappeared through the compartment and then, with the curtain half-open, we could see her in deep discussion with the airline help in the back of the plane.

The other stewardess in the front cabin advised us to put up our trays and was furtively snatching up anything lying around the premises. The seatbelt sign came on and the plane seemed to pivot in another direction. Clearly something was wrong. Herb turned to me, asking the logical question about what I thought had happened. Always prepared with an answer, I said either they had just found out there was a fire in the plane or they had been informed there was a bomb on board. The plane was obviously losing altitude. I ventured that the pilot was probably looking for the nearest place to land.

With that I reached into my inside pocket and took out a canceled envelope and began to write down several columns of figures. Peering over my shoulder, Herb demanded, "What the hell are you doing?" "Herb," I explained, "if anything happens to this plane, I have to be the prime suspect." I told him I had stopped in the airport and bought the maximum amount of insurance allowed.

"But what are those figures you jotted down there?" he urged, in some confusion. I replied that if Jean sought the advice of Jerry Hoffberger and he suggested something of an investment that produced 4 percent or 5 percent annually, I wanted to figure out how much she and our seven kids would have to live on, plus, of course, my life insurance and our other small investments. "But Frank," he scolded, "I'm supposed to be doing that kind of thing. You're supposed to be praying. You're supposed to be praying to save this plane from going down." There were a few minutes of serious silence, then I began to laugh. He did, too, and the laugh seemed to break the spell.

We sat back and waited for the inevitable. The laugh had scuttled our silent fears as the plane settled into an even more precipitous descent. Minutes went by, which seemed like hours. Then we landed in what first appeared to be an open field. But that was impossible; I quickly persuaded myself that empty fields don't {177 have runways or landing strips. It became obvious that we were at the far end of a runway at some airport, somewhere, but not in Detroit, our ultimate destination. Then my thought processes were interrupted by the stewardesses urging us to hurry off the plane through an open door near the cockpit. It seemed to be the same way we had got on the plane a short time before.

Safely on the ground, all of our guesses were uncannily correct. We were at the end of the farthest runway at the Cleveland Airport. The plane was surrounded by fire trucks, ambulances, police vehicles, and airport personnel. They were all prepared for a major disaster. We were quickly directed to a site in the terminal manned by uniformed police personnel, who interviewed each and every one of the passengers. We also were told we were in Cleveland and no reason was given for the interruption of our travel plans. But airline officials were just outside to give us help in getting to Detroit and beyond.

Helen Delich Bentley, then a maritime reporter for the *Baltimore Morning Sun* and later a U.S. congresswoman from Baltimore, was on the flight and we later learned the full story from her newspaper account. A pair of National Guard soldiers had done their summer stint of active duty in Maryland. Before heading home, they had spent the previous night at the home of a soldier buddy. They left the next morning to head to Baltimore's Friendship Airport. Their host the previous night had a couple of young children with active imaginations. They had discussed among themselves what would happen if the two military men carried a live bomb onto their plane on the flight home. Somehow they convinced themselves that this was a real possibility, and even though they knew it was past departure time, they called authorities and reported that the two soldiers were toting bombs and planning to blow up the plane.

This, of course, set off an immediate alarm. First, a simple phone call confirmed that two servicemen had boarded the plane. Then the flight crew was warned. With the warning came the instruction to get the plane on the ground as soon as possible. Where? That was left up to the pilot, and the officials fervently hoped he had some knowledge of where he was going. The veteran pilot chose nearby Cleveland, a venue he had flown into many times. He so informed his crew and headquarters advised the target airport, which swung into action with preparations for the emergency landing and a possible unthinkable disaster. In my opinion, they all did a masterful job and I was grateful.

Mets Changes

Getting back to the Mets, there was another significant event that unfolded after the 1986 World Series. Doubleday & Company, which, under Nelson Doubleday, was the principal owner of the Mets franchise, sold its publishing company to Bertelsmann, the worldwide German media giant. Of course, part of Doubleday publishing was the New York Mets. Baseball rules precluded a foreign company from owning a franchise, so the Mets were immediately for sale.

Nelson was anxious to buy the club for his own personal interest, with the price reported to be $100 million. Considering that the club had been purchased for a reported record $21 million six years earlier, the new price—almost five times greater—seemed eminently fair.

As it was explained to me, Fred Wilpon, the minority partner who had put the original deal together back in 1980, then brought forth a relevant legal document. This established that, if the club were ever sold, Wilpon had the first option to purchase. All the would-be partners had agreed to this when the club was originally acquired from the Payson family. To be honest, I never fully understood how that legal paper ever survived the due diligence inspection by the purchasing partners. It authorized an individual who had only a reported 5 percent of the team to have the sole option to purchase if the team was ever sold.

Wilpon exercised his option to buy, but in what I saw as a conciliatory move on his part, he offered half the team back to

Doubleday. They made the deal and Wilpon and Doubleday became co-owners of the Mets.

All of these latest maneuvers proved to be a major puzzle to me. I had a great working relationship with Doubleday. I ran the club and kept him up to date on what was going on. He preferred it that way. So did I, and thus we got along famously. After the sales, I met with both partners, Doubleday and Wilpon, individually and then together. In all instances I was assured that nothing was going to change. I was to have complete control of the franchise. That meant producing a final financial figure every year and a line-by-line report to the ownership.

I constantly advised the owners that the whole operational game consisted entirely of four letters: W and L (wins and losses) and P and L (profit and loss), and these factors were integrated and synergized each other.

180 } One thing did happen that I didn't give much thought to until years later, when Wilpon started to have financial difficulties. When Doubleday had first sought to hire me in 1980, I agreed to his conditions as long as I had complete control of the ball club. We had a short but interesting conversation. He promised me "no problem" about running the club. In putting the whole deal together, Fred, at his request, was given a two-year tenure as the president of the club, and Doubleday, who had no interest in titles, nevertheless became chairman of the board, with me as executive VP and general manager. But in two years, Nelson specified, I was to take over the presidential slot.

I had really forgotten about the whole matter when about a year and ten months into the job, Fred made an appointment to see me and hinted that he had a special favor to ask. When we got together, Fred, indeed, was looking for a favor. Prior to claiming the slot as president, he confessed there were not a lot of big doors being opened to him in the New York real estate business. At the time, he was just a small time player, mostly on the commercial side. Wilpon said, "Once I began to visit the banks and lending institutions as president of the Mets, things changed drastically and I had no trouble in getting loans and other breaks for my personal real estate business."

Then he asked me if I would step aside and allow him to remain as president of the Mets. "It means a lot to me and my family," he explained, adding, "I certainly wouldn't interfere in any way with the ball club." Titles meant nothing to me, and as long as I was left alone to build a winning organization, I would be happy. I granted his wish and Fred remained president. Subsequently, I asked him a couple of times, "How is it going?" Inevitably, I got back an affirmative and cheerful reply. Things appeared to be going well for his real estate business. And it was none of my concern, I constantly reminded myself.

True to his word, Wilpon never had a word to say about how we ran the ball club, not surprising since Doubleday had 95 percent ownership until the organization was completely rebuilt and had won a World Series in 1986. Even after he and Nelson became joint owners following the '86 season, as they promised, I was left completely alone to direct the baseball operation. That's the way it remained until I retired five years later.

Since Fred was the president of the club, I always felt it was my duty to keep him informed about what was happening with the team. So, just as I kept Nelson advised on the baseball goings-on, I similarly briefed Wilpon. Thus, when they became joint owners, my duties didn't change.

To my memory, the subject of investing money with investment manager Bernie Madoff came up only once during my tenure. While Wilpon invested some of his personal holdings with Madoff, Doubleday declined to participate and, thereby, nixed any placement of Mets funds at that time. Long after I had retired and Wilpon had bought out Doubleday and became the sole owner of the Mets, these financial matters changed drastically. Madoff became a major player in the Mets' financial picture as the Mets started to invest considerable money with his company. In 2008, when Madoff's operation was exposed as a giant, illegal Ponzi scheme, Wilpon's operations at the Mets came under fire. The Mets' legal and financial problems piled up. Loans were secured from MLB and Bank of America to shore up the shaky situation amid rumors the team might be up for sale.

After the Mets became winners in the mid-1980s, Wilpon, as president of the Mets, was given credit by a lot of the media for remaking the New York Mets into a contender. He never hesitated to take the bows. In experiencing this, I was not unmindful of what had happened to me in Baltimore. Truly, the Orioles were a well-built club when I got there and ready to win it all. No effort necessary on my part. Starting with the 1966 season, we were in four World Series in the next six seasons mostly with the basic talent that GM Lee MacPhail had put together. But I did take many of the bows.

30

New Choices

With the Mets having won 108 games during the regular 1986 season and a subsequent World Series, it appeared that the team would be a contender for the rest of the 1980s. And it was. That club had been put together to last awhile. We had two budding superstars in Gooden and Strawberry. There was a good mixture of old and young players and the pitching staff was predominantly young. More championships seemed likely. Ironically, it was the young part that turned out to be a disappointment.

Gooden seemed to be unable to cope with the New York version of the "in crowd." Straw was being consistently persuaded by his agent that the grass (literally and figuratively) was greener on the other side of the fence, particularly in LA. So in 1991 Straw cut his ties to the Mets and joined the LA Dodgers. It was not money that made the difference; it was his agent's dream of the player becoming an instant movie star and a heavy in show business.

After returning to LA, his hometown, and testing the waters, Straw couldn't wait to get back to New York. He did so in 1995, when George Steinbrenner brought him to the Yankees. In his seventeen seasons in the Majors, Straw had some good years and averaged thirty-four home runs a season, but he never hit over .300, and he fell short of the tremendous potential that many of us saw in the early '80s.

Gooden, who had been suspected of using drugs, owned up to it and spent some time going in and out of rehab. But he never was the same pitcher. (In fact, several of our young athletes were charmed by the New York "cowboys" and the team was the worse for it.) Over sixteen seasons in the Majors, Gooden compiled a winning won-lost record of 194-112. Following the '86 World Series victory, Doc had some very good years in the late '80s and early '90s with the Mets, but then he fell off dramatically. After being out of baseball for two years, he signed with the Yankees in 1996. The rest of his career, with several teams, was undistinguished. Over his full career, Doc's only twenty-game winning season was in 1985 when he was an amazing 24-4 with the Mets. Doc was good, no doubt, but many of us had much higher career expectations for him.

In short, we were let down by ballplayers who chose to use illegal substances. Despite these disappointments and, perhaps, missed opportunities for more glory, the 1980s was the decade of the Mets. In that ten-year span, the Mets won more games— 814—than any other Major League club. What was more important to the bottom line, they drew greater attendance than any other team in baseball, drawing more than three million fans to Shea Stadium in both 1987 and 1988 and coming close to that mark in three other years.

It's been said that when the Great Scorer up above puts the final mark behind your name, it's not whether you won or lost but how many fans paid to see the game.

After the '86 success I began to think about getting out of baseball and going back to my old dreams. I had promised Nelson Doubleday that I would rebuild his newly purchased team into a contender and win back fan support to prevent a financial disaster. And I kept my promise.

Actually, I might have missed out on savoring the 1986 championship if certain events had gone differently a year before. Since I ran one of the divisions of Doubleday & Company, the baseball team which I referred to as "The Fun and Games Department," I attended the company board meetings whenever they occurred. One of these was the annual Doubleday company meeting, which was held in some interesting spots. I particularly remember one that took place in Barbados. I always spent some time preparing my "Fun and Games" report, with the emphasis on the "Fun" part.

I was an avid reader, going back to my newspaper days, maybe even to college or high school. For as long as I can remember, books were an important part of my life. Ernest Hemingway was my number one favorite writer. I had read all of his novels more than once, as well as his short stories.

Early on, the Doubleday editors knew of my proclivities and sent me a small number of books, seeking my opinion. Mostly they were books built around sport, not all but a majority. *The Legend of Bagger Vance*, about a down-and-out golfer, was one book that stuck with me. Most of the manuscripts I marked up were well worth publishing, though I didn't hit home runs on all of those sent my way. I distinctly remember returning *Forrest Gump* with a note that proclaimed it was one of the worst books I had ever read and certainly not worth publishing. Fortunately, the powers at the top paid no attention to me and published the book that, everyone knows, ultimately became a highly successful movie. Tom Hanks and his box of chocolates is what I remember most of the flick. In my defense, it seemed to me that there were many changes between novel and movie script. The book sold very well after the movie came out.

I was somewhat astonished when, in the mid-1980s, John O'Donnell, the chief financial officer at Doubleday, invited me to lunch, and after some preliminary sparring asked me if I had ever considered going to work for Doubleday & Company in their publishing end. He quickly added that the entire Doubleday board was impressed with what I had done with the ball team, but they were interested in me as their new top editor—a very important job, he informed me. When I asked the inevitable question, "Why me?" he said that they were thinking about bringing in someone from outside for the job. They were impressed with my leadership and a host of other things. He didn't actually make the job offer, but did ask me to consider it and seemed to indicate it was mine if I wanted it.

What would happen to my ball club if I bailed now? That was the first question I asked myself. Were Al Harazin and Joe McIlvanie ready to step up a rung? This was not something I had anticipated considering for a long time. Talk to your wife, was my next thought. Make up your mind. It should come as no surprise that I was anxious to talk to my wife. Husbands who are looking to change jobs usually consult their wives. Besides, the lovely Jean and I had been married more than forty years at the time and had seven children, five boys first and then two girls. A basketball team and two cheerleaders, is the way I used to laughingly describe it. Along with a basketful of charms, Jean was what I would describe as levelheaded. She dispensed good advice. Inevitably she would give me thoughts on both sides of the problem and then her feelings on a solution. But that was always followed by "Whatever you want to do, Frank, whatever makes you happy." What a woman!

186 }

Baseball made me happy. I had suffered through the early years and now the club was on the verge of winning. I surely wanted to be around for that. Calling O'Donnell to thank him for the luncheon and the conversation, I found him sympathetic to my desire to stick with baseball, and the matter of the editor job never came up again. A couple of years later when Doubleday & Company was sold to Bertelsmann, I wondered where I would have bounced to if I had chosen the book route.

In 1987 Davey Johnson's forces won ninety-two games and were in the thick of the pennant race while finishing in second place behind the Cardinals in the NL East. In 1988, when the Mets posted one hundred victories to win the East and set up a league championship match with the LA Dodgers, the Mets drew a record-setting 3,047,724 fans during the regular season, and it looked like "all was right with the world."

There was a flock of new marks that year. Johnson became the first National League manager to win more than ninety games in each of his first five years in the league. Strawberry would hit a record-matching thirty-nine home runs in '88. Gooden won eighteen games and Darling, seventeen. A couple of good recent trades also enhanced the 1988 season. The trades brought pitcher David Cone, who achieved a 20-3 record to lead a great pitching staff, and outfielder Kevin McReynolds, who had 99 RBIs and 21 stolen bases. It had been a scintillating season, but the Dodgers made it less than perfect with a four-games-to-three win in the playoffs. It was a bitter series with the fourth game going twelve innings. Dodgers ace Orel Hershiser shut out the Mets, 6–0, in the finale.

Johnson was around as Mets manager until 1990, when he developed the bad habit of clashing with owners in his public statements. But his success with his ball clubs remained unabated. Moving from New York, he did a short stint with Marge Schott { 187 and the Cincinnati Reds. From there it was to our old ball club, the Baltimore Orioles, where he was the most successful leader since Earl Weaver and had the O's at the top of the class only to draw the wrath of owner Peter Angelos over the fate of some charitable contributions. The latter, however minor it may have seemed, cost Johnson his job in what I personally considered to be one of the stupidest things the Baltimore ownership could've done as the club began to spiral downward.

Davey moved on to the LA Dodgers as their manager before tiring of the frequent moves and opting to stay on the sidelines. His managerial days after the Mets were very successful. Under his tutelage both the Reds and the Orioles made it to league championships. He was not as fortunate with the Dodgers. After his departure from LA, Davey served as a consultant to Major League clubs and dabbled in international baseball while handling the Netherlands' national team in the Olympics. He was lured back to managing the Washington Nationals in 2011 after their manager unexpectedly quit in midseason. The Johnson magic worked again, and in 2012 Davey's Nats made the National League playoffs and he was named NL manager of the year.

Davey and I may share the same emotions about Shea Stadium. We both were on the winning side, he as manager, in the Mets' win over the Red Sox in 1986. Both of us were on the losing side in that same stadium in 1969, when the Mets upset our Orioles. Davey, then the Orioles second baseman, had the distinction of making the last out of that upset series, flying out against Mets pitcher Jerry Koosman. For me, being inducted into the Mets Hall of Fame in 2009 was a special honor, made even more special by a reunion with the other three inductees—Davey Johnson, Darryl Strawberry, and Dwight Gooden.

After losing in the playoffs in 1988, second place was the Mets' lot for the next two years. In 1991, my final year at the helm, we fell back to fifth place to break a seven-year streak of first- or second-place finishes. It was time for me to go.

188 }

My early business training in Baltimore under Jerry Hoffberger had taught me that any time you grab a top-rated job, you should facilitate a line of succession—so that if you decided to go elsewhere or if your current company kicked you upstairs, there were ready replacements. That was only fair to your current employers. In the business world, it's an old axiom that a CEO's most important job is picking his or her successor. I gave it much thought. As previously mentioned, Al Harazin had been my number one guy both in New York and in Baltimore. I considered him to be the best all-around baseball executive I'd ever known. I had absolutely no doubt that he could take over the business part of the whole organization and run it superbly.

Joe McIlvanie, who also had worked for me in Baltimore and New York in a variety of slots, was ready to head up all the ball-player functions under Harazin's direction. I was secure knowing there would be a dynamic duo in place whenever I decided to go back to eating hard crabs and oysters and living by Florida beaches and the waterways of Chesapeake Bay.

31

Extra Innings

To inject a few random thoughts at this closing stage of the narrative, let me say that I had discovered I was a dinosaur in the sport. When I came into professional baseball in the mid-1960s, the top executive was the general manager. He was in charge of everything. He was what they called in the business dynamic the COO. In the past, the general manager headed up the whole operation and was directly responsible for the entire operation. But a change was imminent. You could see it coming.

Currently, the general manager is responsible only for the baseball operations. Somebody else handles stadium operations, the field, the ground crew, and the like. And still others handle financial matters, concessions, and ticket sales. A true GM, in my book, also heads up the scouting staff and the Minor League operations in addition to the Major League club.

My succession plans went awry when McIlvanie succumbed to the San Diego Padres' lure of a general managership while I was still heading up the Mets. Harazin was around to succeed me after the 1990 season but was only given a two-year shot at the top spot before the club re-signed McIlvanie as the chief executive and handed Al his walking papers. I had agreed to hang around for an additional year, 1991, but was of scant help in the transition. So, in 1992, Jean and I left the New York area and returned to Maryland, this time settling across the Chesapeake Bay in the town of Easton, and divided our time between Maryland and Florida, where we also had a home.

The Mets fell below .500 for successive seasons and continued to struggle into the mid-1990s under a series of field managers—Bud Harrelson, Mike Cubbage, Jeff Torborg, and then Dallas Green, a veteran who finally gave way to Bobby Valentine and general manager Steve Phillips. The latter came out of our Minor League system and worked his way up the ladder.

I had some reservations about Steve as a player after we first drafted him. A very intelligent young man out of high school in Detroit, he was offered a full ride to college at Northwestern with sports teams and through scholarships. A slick quarterback in football, Steve looked to be a college star in the making. In baseball he was a better-than-average infielder and certainly good enough to be drafted and given a shot at professional baseball. But he put the college path aside and signed with the Mets organization.

After three years in the Minors, it became apparent that Steve was not Major League playing material. At this point, we began to talk about an idea we had discussed a few years earlier. That was, if Steve was interested, to move him into an administrative slot in the front office. This meant he would start as an assistant in some part of the Minor League system. I was still calling the shots and had been impressed with Steve. While still playing baseball in the Minors, he had gone back to school in the off-season and was close to getting his college degree from the University of Michigan. He had also found a lovely and talented girl, Marci, at Ann Arbor, and had married her and started a family.

Although Steve took off the uniform with a good deal of reluctance, he agreed to give up his playing career for a job as assistant to the Minor League farm director. He moved up the ladder in quick but measured steps, and when there was a need for the top baseball spot, he became general manager in 1997, with Bobby Valentine in the dugout as his manager. The Mets won the National League pennant in 2000, but in the turn-of-the-century World Series they lost to their fellow New Yorkers, the Yankees.

After a couple of years managing in the big show, Valentine

went off to Japan, where he was eminently successful in guiding a team to the pennant in that country. He was the best teacher of the game I ever encountered, and I always considered him a top-flight professional. Somehow, though, he always seemed unable to get along with owners. Valentine got back into the Majors when he managed the Boston Red Sox in 2012 but was let go at the end of the season.

Steve Phillips, on the other hand, had too many extracurricular activities with the ladies in the parent firm—and some out of the firm—which brought about his sad demise in the baseball business. After that, he had a very promising start in the sports reporting business, but he succumbed to a similar weakness and that attractive door again slammed shut. After the subway fall classic between the Mets and Yankees in 2000, Steve graciously assigned me a World Series ring. By this time I had been retired eight years and had little to do with the club. I was touched by { 191 his thoughtfulness.

You know, baseball is all about rings. In every professional league, the champion in the circuit gets rings. Top to bottom, throughout the professional baseball leagues, the champion is awarded rings, some less ostentatious than others, of course, but the effect is the same. Getting to the World Series is the big one. The winners get the big World Series finger jewelry. The losers are entitled to a copy, though a less demonstrative one, because, after all, they won their league, didn't they? Needless to say, they conveniently call it a World Series ring.

Down through the years, I had accumulated a couple handfuls of rings and a passel of world champion editions. Since Jean and I have five sons, I decided to pass the rings on to them while I was still on the scene rather than waiting until my demise. We distributed the rings in 1993. Our oldest boy, Greg, got first pick, and the remaining were distributed in chronological order. Greg took the '86 Mets ring. When our fifth son, Sean, got his turn, he seized the first generation of an Orioles-winning World Series ring. By the way, none of my five sons played on a baseball team; all were lacrosse players.

Jean and I were able to combine our love of family and Ireland by taking all seven children on a two-week trip to the Emerald Island to celebrate our fiftieth wedding anniversary. It would be for all of them, and to make things easier, all were invited to bring their spouses. No grandchildren were stipulated, in order to give their parents fourteen days of unencumbered pleasure.

A charter bus trip from Baltimore to New York got lost attempting to find Kennedy Airport and we arrived just in time for the scheduled flight overseas. This caused a lot of anxiety among the newly traveling bunch. Shortly thereafter, things got even more unsettled with the announcement that the scheduled flight was postponed to an unscheduled time since the plane had been ruled unable to make the journey, and a different aircraft was being flown in to take its place.

The airport bar looked like some form of release from all of the pent-up emotions, and the fifteen-person Cashen traveling party headed in that direction. It emerged more than two hours later with a $200 bar bill and tramped onto an older and slower plane for the overseas journey.

With this single exception, the trip was an unqualified success. We had hired the same driver-guide, Colin Dardis, that we had used for the golf tours. He had a comfortable sixteen-seat Mercedes van and an attached trailer that carried the luggage. Everyone was limited to one travel bag and no golf clubs so the load was not unmanageable. As seasoned travelers to Ireland, Jean and I had decided to forgo a daily bus tour over the length and breadth of the country and, instead, selected three destinations in the Republic of Ireland in which to spend time. We felt this would give our children a good idea of what Ireland was really like.

The first stop was Adare, a picturesque little spot in the middle of the country and a village of old-time, thatched-roof cottages that was frequently voted the prettiest in the country. It was a small journey out of Adare for the children to see where their grandparents were born in Tipperary.

Greg and Terry discovered a riding stable and talked their brothers and sisters into joining them and their spouses on a trail ride. From what I was told, Greg, the oldest of the Cashen children, assumed he was John Wayne and insisted on leading the pack and giving the needed signals. It was so much fun that they all repeated the feat when we moved on to the next stop and found another riding stable.

After that it was off to Dingle Peninsula, where we examined the nautical magic of the country, including the fishing industry and some of the remote and ancient islands off the coast. For the final third of our visit we went to Killarney, my favorite, and took the children to stay at Killen House, where Michael and Geraldine Rosney preside over a great, small hotel with an equally great restaurant that also contains what I consider to be the best bar { 193 in the world. The bar is known as the Ball Room, where the walls are covered with interesting golf balls from all kinds of distant places. Of equal import is the dark Guinness beer being drawn from nearby kegs. Your drinks were sometimes counted in Roman numerals posted on a wall board.

Four more days of nonstop celebration at the Killen House left the Cashen crew ready to go home. The plane trip to New York came off with a lot less fuss than the journey over entailed. As you may have garnered from my litany on the subject, Ireland is a source of great pleasure. The food, particularly the seafood, is excellent and the golf courses are among the world's best. But jobs in Ireland are scarce and financially the country is frequently close to collapse, and the immigration numbers among the young and well educated are much too high.

What have I learned from my crazy journey through the baseball wars? It's a question I frequently ask myself, and it usually brings on a flood of disjointed thoughts. To get it straight, I used to imagine that nighttime maven David Letterman had invited me to appear on his show and asked for my list of ten things a GM should know. That caused me to make the list that follows, and to take Gene Autry's old advice by "checking it twice."

Number 10: Never let your team grow old together.

Number 9: Have the courage of your own convictions.

Number 8: Ballplayers don't learn to win in the Majors; they learn to win in the Minors.

Number 7: There are ballplayers you win with and ballplayers you lose with; it doesn't always depend on ERA (pitchers' earned run average) or BA (hitters' batting average).

Number 6: The four letters that really describe and dissect the team are "W" and "L" and "P" and "L"—Wins and Losses and Profit and Loss. There is a strange but constant synergy among them.

Number 5: Know both the strengths and the weaknesses of your employees.

Number 4: Scouts are some of the most important but least recognized people in the game.

Number 3: A good and productive Minor League system is a must.

Number 2: You can never have too much left-handed pitching.

Number 1: Pitching is 65 percent of the game.